STUCKEY

STUCKEY

The Biography of Williamson Sylvester Stuckey 1909–1977

By
Elizabeth McCants Drinnon

Mercer University Press
Macon, Georgia
—1997—

Isbn 0.86554.569.3
MUP.H425

Stuckey
The Biography of Williamson Sylvester Stuckey
by Elizabeth McCants Drinnon

Mercer University Press
6316 Peake Road
Macon, Georgia 31210-3960

Photograph Credit: Stuckey Scrapbook, Sidney Ridley, Everett Drinnon, Jack Lott, Lynda Stuckey Franklin.

The paper used in this publication meets the minimum requirements of American National Standard for Information Sciences—Permanence of Paper for Printed Library Materials, ANSI Z39.48–1984.

Library of Congress Cataloging-in-Publication Data

Drinnon, Elizabeth McCants.
Stuckey: the biography of Williamson Sylvester Stuckey / by Elizabeth McCants Drinnon
p. cm.
Includes bibliographical references.
ISBN 0-86554-569-3 (alk. paper)
1. Stuckey, Williamson Sylvester, 1910-1977
2. Restaurateurs—United States—Biography. 3. Grocers—United States—Biography. 4. Fast Food restaurants—United States—History. 5. Convenience stores—United States—History. I. Title.
TX910.5.S78D75 1997
647.95'092—dc21
[B] 97-29743
CIP

TABLE OF CONTENTS

ACKNOWLEDGMENT

Lynda Stuckey Franklin wishes to express deep appreciation to Ethelynn McMillan Stuckey for her valuable assistance with family reminiscences and memorabilia, and to Elva Lee Connell for her inestimable help with recalling the day to day operation of Stuckey's. Special recognition and thanks also go to members of the Stuckey family and to many friends for sharing their memories of Williamson Sylvester Stuckey.

Preface

The biography of Williamson Sylvester Stuckey—or "Stuckey" as he was known—has been written for the purpose of recording his remarkable life story for his descendants. This work is intended to serve as a reminder of the unique legacy that belongs to Stuckey's children, grandchildren, great-grandchildren, and to future generations of the family. Their heritage, as descendants of a man who parlayed a borrowed $35 into a multi-million dollar chain that stretched from coast to coast, is to be cherished. This year, 1997, marking the twentieth anniversary of his death, is an appropriate time for the publication of "Stuckey."

Despite his many accomplishments as an entrepreneur, a marketing expert, and a philanthropist, Stuckey was first and foremost a devoted family man whose influence is still strongly felt today by those he loved. This book is written for the two of us fortunate to know him as "Daddy," and for those who lovingly called him "Big Daddy," as well as for those generations yet to come. All will have this book as tangible evidence of the life of a man who answered to the name of simply "Stuckey."

—Lynda Stuckey Franklin
July 1997

Chapter One

THE STAGE IS SET

"How much farther is it to Stuckey's?" Sammy whines.

"Yeah—how long till we get there, Dad?" grumbles Suzy.

Long-suffering Dad, driving this hot July day in 1954 on U.S. 341, winding across South Georgia, headed eventually to the beach at St. Simons Island, wipes perspiration from his brow before he replies:

"That last billboard said it's twenty miles. Didn't you see it?"

"But, Dad-dee, I can't wait to see the parrot," whines Suzy. "And I'm thirsty, too, and Sammy just pinched me. Besides, it's hot in the back seat."

"It's hot in the front seat, too, Suzy," laments Dad, "but hold on. We'll soon be at Stuckey's."

"See, there's another billboard already," Mom exclaims. "And now it's only twelve miles to Stuckey's. We can go in and cool off—they're air conditioned."

"Puh-leeze hurry, Dad. I've got to go to the bathroom real bad," chirps Sammy.

"Those cursed billboards drive me nuts," Dad says.

"They work, though, don't they?" asks Mom. "You couldn't possibly pass by Stuckey's in Eastman now without stopping, could you? There'll probably be two or three more gentle reminders before we get there. And, besides, where else can you find good clean rest rooms?"

"You're right," agrees Dad. "I might as well fill up the tank with gasoline while I'm there, too. That'll make it one less stop."

"And I want to get some pralines and maybe some fudge. And I can't wait to see the parrot and hear him say, 'hello' and 'hey there,'" exclaims Suzy.

"Why don't you read one of your comic books aloud, Sammy?" suggests Mom. "We'll be there soon, and it will help to pass the time."

"Look!" shouts Suzy. "There's another billboard coming up—Hooray! Only five miles now to Stuckey's."

"Whoever dreamed up the idea for billboards sure knows how to build up suspense," comments Dad. "Darned if there's not one around just about every curve now."

"Stuckey's, Stuckey's, Stuckey's. We can't wait till we get to Stuckey's," chime Suzy and Sammy in unison, over and over.

"I see one just around the next curve, Dad," shouts Sammy. "It's three miles to Stuckey's. Only three more miles, three more miles, three more miles."

"Well, look at that," exclaims Mom. "Your waiting is about over. Surely this is the last one of the blasted things—five hundred yards to Stuckey's."

"We're here! We're here! We're at Stuckey's," exclaim Suzy and Sammy together.

"Thank God," breathes Dad.

This typical family of the period stops at Stuckey's, fills the automobile tank, has the radiator checked, adds a quart of oil, uses the spotlessly clean rest rooms, says hello to the store's resident parrot, quenches their thirst with soft drinks, buys a bag of pralines, divinity and pecan log rolls, and a few souvenirs for good measure, plus a jar of jelly for Grandma.

By stopping at Stuckey's, they had joined thousands of other tourists who succumbed to the enticing messages on more than 4,000 billboards promoting the more than 350

Stuckey's stores across the country at the height of the Stuckey chain's success.

Stuckey's, though ostensibly selling candy and pecans, actually provided a one-stop, all-inclusive service, a rarity in the days before convenience stores, self-serve gasoline pumps, fast food outlets, and interstate highways. The enticement of a parrot or mynah bird in each store was icing on the cake—an added attraction which children loved and parents endured.

The phenomenal success story of Williamson Sylvester Stuckey is straight from the pages of Horatio Alger. Born in Dodge County, Georgia, on March 26, 1909, he was the first child of his parents, William Ira Stuckey and Sallie Lee Williamson Stuckey. His first name, Williamson, was the maiden name of his mother. Stuckey was later joined by a brother, Felix Jay Stuckey, born on November 9, 1915. The Stuckey boys grew up on the family farm in the way most boys grew up on South Georgia farms in those days, learning what was considered most important—the back-breaking hard work necessary to keep an unmechanized farm operation going.

As the oldest son, young Stuckey learned to plow a straight furrow with a stubborn mule, to keep up with the best pickers of the white fluffy bolls of cotton, and to suffer bleeding hands, the occupational hazard all good fodder pullers knew well. Young Stuckey slopped the hogs and milked the cows at ungodly hours long before the first streaks of day lighted Dodge County's eastern sky. Hard labor was the expected way of life for the young Stuckey boys, just as it was for almost all of their friends and acquaintances.

There was one difference, however, that Sylvester Stuckey (as he was called in his early years) experienced. His parents believed in the importance of education and insisted that he and his brother not only attend the public schools of Dodge County, but also that they apply themselves diligently to their studies. There was another difference, too, one which was to influence Sylvester's entire life. He was blessed with a remarkable grandmother, Cora Powell Williamson, a strong-willed, determined woman. She underscored his parents' emphasis on education, and believed that his potential for success was unlimited. She openly expressed her belief in her young grandson often.

When young Stuckey's mother, Sallie Williamson Stuckey, died on September 21, 1923, at the age of thirty-four, he was fourteen years old. His Grandmother Williamson became the maternal figure and dominant influence in his life. Although he continued to work for his father, it was his Grandmother Williamson who provided the strong guidance for his life. The traits of good character, honesty and trustworthiness were instilled in him early, and by example he learned a work ethic which would remain with him throughout his life.

Research into the Stuckey family genealogy and its related branches, conducted primarily by Anne Stuckey Clarke of Atlanta, Georgia (the daughter of the late Felix Jay Stuckey), shows a strong indication that the Stuckey family name originated in Switzerland, although at least one reference leans toward a French origin. Mrs. Clarke believes that, since the Swiss government did not allow its citizens to emigrate to America, many went via Holland, England, and other countries. Since France borders on Switzerland, this might easily explain the French origin.

Mrs. Clarke's research shows that Stuckeys have been in England for centuries, particularly in the Devon area, as well as in other parts of the British Isles. One source shows that Simon Stuckey (a brother of John, probable ancestors of the Dodge County Stuckey family) married a Scottish woman on the ship coming to America. Family legend, however, has it that the family came to America from Ireland. Genealogists know that people often tarried briefly in a new country before emigration to the New World. Mrs. Clarke's research is in progress and is, therefore, incomplete at present.

As with most family surnames, there are variations in spellings. It is believed that the Dodge County Stuckey line originated with the emigration of John "Stuckee" to Philadelphia in 1735. He was then joined by his brothers,

Simon and Jacob Stookey/Stuckey. Some family members later settled in Virginia and South Carolina.

Although Mrs. Clarke is still seeking final verification of some details, she believes that the Stuckey line leading to her father, Felix Jay Stuckey, and to her uncles, Williamson Sylvester Stuckey and Frank Stuckey (their half brother) has been established from Simon Stuckey (the immigrant) who died in 1759-60. His appraisal report listed orphaned sons Edmund and Simon Stuckey on the Isle of Wight, Virginia. Edmund was born in 1745 and died in 1831. Edmund Stuckey's son, Simon, was born November 12, 1769; the date of death has not yet been established. Simon Stuckey's son, Starling Stuckey, was born in 1790, and lived in Wilkinson County, Georgia, and died in 1838. Starling's son, John Stuckey, born October 21, 1823, resided in Wilkinson County also, and was a Confederate soldier, serving in Co. F, 2nd Ga. Infantry, Georgia State Line, and died May 4, 1908. He is buried in the Orphans Cemetery in Eastman. John Stuckey was the father of John Franklin Stuckey, who was born June 23, 1856, and died June 23, 1922, also buried in the Orphans Cemetery. John Franklin Stuckey was the father of William Ira Stuckey, who was born September 17, 1883, and his death occurred on December 24, 1951, in Dodge County.

This research represents nine generations of the Stuckey family in America, up to and including the generation of Williamson Sylvester Stuckey. With the additions of his children, grandchildren and great-grandchildren, three more generations are added, for a total of twelve generations of the family.

Mrs. Clarke's research reflects various branches of the family, married into by ancestors in the Stuckey line, including Carr, Powell, Joiner, Brazeal, Flowers, Mann, Powers, Thomas, Taylor, Kinchen, Butler, Howell, and Williamson.

Although it is not practical here to go into the established ancestry of these various maternal lines, the known information on the Williamson family is included. The mother of Williamson Sylvester Stuckey, Sallie Lee Williamson, was born September 10, 1889. She died on September 21, 1923, at the young age of 34. She was the daughter of Felix Williamson, April 8, 1866–February 8, 1910, and Cora Lee Powell Williamson, January 8, 1872–July 3, 1953. Both are buried in the Orphans Cemetery in Eastman. (It was Mrs. Williamson who reared Sallie's two sons, Williamson Sylvester and Felix Jay.)

Felix Williamson was the son of Doctor Felix Williamson (1810-12–1866) and Evaline Joiner Williamson (1812–1866) of Columbus County, North Carolina. ("Doctor" was a first-name, not a title.) Doctor Felix Williamson was the son of Lott Williamson, born in 1790 and died in 1860, married to Hannah Flowers Williamson (1792–1860), and living in Columbus County, North Carolina. Also established are the Powell and Kinchen lines through Mrs. Cora Lee Powell Williamson, grandmother of Williamson Sylvester Stuckey.

Thus, it is clear that Williamson Sylvester Stuckey was descended from generations of solid community-minded citizens, many of whom were teachers, and many prosperous in agricultural pursuits, as well as many large land owners. A number of ancestors, in addition to his great-grandfather, John Stuckey, also served in the Confederacy.

An example of the esteem in which many of the family members were held is recorded in the life of James Jarrett Kinchen in *Memoirs of Georgia,* published in 1895 by The Southern Historical Association in Atlanta, Georgia. Kinchen's biographical sketch shows that he was a teacher in Pulaski County, Georgia, for 35 years, and a large plantation owner. His grandfather, William Kinchen, of North Carolina, was a patriot in the Revolutionary War. Cora Powell Williamson's mother was Sarah Elizabeth Kinchen (1852-1897), the daughter of James Jarrett Kinchen.

The historic Orphans Cemetery two miles northwest of Eastman is the resting place for the recent generations of Williamson Sylvester Stuckey's ancestors, both Stuckeys and Williamsons. The cemetery, established by Albert Gould Williamson, has an interesting history. Six Williamson brothers, including Doctor Felix Williamson, came as orphans and early pioneer settlers from North Carolina to Dodge County in the 1870's. The brothers were affectionately known as the "Orphans." When Albert Gould donated land for the cemetery and a church across the road, they became known as the Orphans in honor of the brothers. In 1912 Albert Gould erected an unusual Georgia marble mausoleum in the cemetery for himself and his wife, Martha J. Buchan Williamson, and a separate single mausoleum was established for his brother, Harmon Havana Williamson. A marble columned canopy adorns the mausoleum which houses a life size sculpture of Mr. and Mrs. Williamson and their nephew, Jay Gould Williamson. The sculpture, done in Italy from Italian marble, attracts a great deal of attention, and visitors from all over the country come to see it. The mausoleums themselves are made of Georgia marble. A Board of Trustees oversees the operation of the cemetery, seeking to continue its operation in the tradition of its first hundred years, and further to preserve it as a historical landmark.

Dodge County is located 55 miles southeast of Macon, Georgia, and Eastman is the county seat. The Williamson farm, on which the Stuckey family lived, is a few miles from the heart of downtown Eastman. Dodge County, with its 431 square miles of rolling, fertile land produced good crops of cotton, corn, peas, peanuts, sweet potatoes, sugar cane, and some tobacco. Although cotton was still king in the first part of the 20th century, most farmers grew other row crops, too. In 1930 Dodge County was ranked fifth in the state in cotton production, with 24,956 bales. The Eastman Cotton Mill was an important industry, providing employment for a large number of persons.

Agriculture, however, was the main industry during the years when young Stuckey was growing up. The population of Dodge County in 1910, the first census after Stuckey's birth, was 20,127, and it changed little with every census until 1940 when a gradual decline in population began. The Ocmulgee River provides the western border of the county between

Dodge and Wilcox Counties, and the county is traversed by the Little Ocmulgee River and a number of streams such as Alligator, Sugar, Mosquito and Gum Creeks. Created by an Act of the Legislature on October 26, 1870, from portions of Laurens, Pulaski, Montgomery and Telfair Counties, Dodge County was named for William E. Dodge. The county was serviced in those days by two railroads, the Seaboard and the Southern.

It was into this typical rural setting that Williamson Sylvester Stuckey was born, firmly backed by generations of solid pioneer ancestors dating to pre-Revolutionary days. The love of the land was inherent in his family, and this was a quality he never outgrew. Indeed, his love affair with the soil would grow stronger as his birthdays passed.

There was little, if anything, in these years to distinguish him from countless other young boys in Dodge County who were expected simply to grow up and follow in their fathers' footsteps. Certainly there was no indication that he was destined to become a multi-millionaire who would change the face of Eastman and Dodge County.

Life in the deep South was not easy in those days. Modern conveniences were nonexistent, but were not missed by those who had never had them. Homes were lighted with kerosene lamps, and only a few had telephones which were housed in wooden cases and operated with a crank. No one had telephone numbers—households were assigned a series of long and short rings, and everyone listened in on everyone else's conversations on the party line in order to keep up with the news. Water came from the well that everyone had in the front yard—only a very few farms boasted windmills. Indoor plumbing did not exist, and every farmhouse had its familiar privy some distance from the house. Horses and buggies, mules and wagons were the main modes of transportation for relatively short distances, and trains if one needed to travel to another state or beyond. As a child, young Stuckey, having nothing with which to compare his lifestyle, no doubt considered it quite normal, that is, if he thought about it at all. And indeed it was normal or typical for that time and place.

Nor did the advent of World War I make much of a difference in his young life, although as an eight-year-old when the United States declared war on Germany in 1917, he would hear his parents discuss the fact that neighbors' sons were putting on uniforms and going off "across the waters" to fight a war that was supposed to end all wars. Everyone was singing George M. Cohan's "Over There," "Pack Up Your Troubles in Your Old Kit Bag," and "Goodbye Broadway, Hello France." Women whose long hair had been considered their crowning glory were bobbing it with great abandon in the shocking new hair style that was sweeping the country.

Young Stuckey knew nothing of the birth of a baby in Brookline, Massachusetts, named John Fitzgerald Kennedy, in 1917, nor did he dream that one day he would head the South Georgia campaign for this baby who would be running for President of the country.

In 1920 the 19th Amendment (known as the Susan B. Anthony Amendment) became a part of the Constitution, and for the first time women had the right to vote. No doubt Stuckey's mother and grandmother were happy to have this new privilege. Meanwhile, the KKK was becoming increasingly violent and active throughout the southern United States, including Georgia.

Slowly progress in transportation became evident in Dodge County and other rural areas of Georgia by the mid to late 1920s. Everyone who could afford it was driving a new Model-T Ford which came in one color, shiny black, complete with running boards and canvas curtains to keep out the rain. No one knew how to drive, and there were many hilarious tales about escapades of the new drivers. Horses, frightened to death of the strange new contraptions, ran away as the cars approached, carrying with them equally frightened passengers in their runaway buggies.

Sadly, there is little evidence that William Ira Stuckey was involved with his sons' upbringing, but there is strong indication that their Grandmother Williamson, a tiny, energetic, wiry woman, long a widow, assumed full responsibility for the two young boys. It is not known what circumstances may have caused the alienation, nor why the two—father and son—lived in Dodge County throughout their lives, with little, if any, contact.

Thus, the early years of Williamson Sylvester Stuckey's youth passed uneventfully.

Chapter 2

PLOWING A STRAIGHT FURROW WITH A STUBBORN MULE

In 1925 at the tender age of sixteen, Sylvester Stuckey was graduated from Dodge County High School. Because he was so young, the family decided that he would stay in high school another year at Eastman High School. Thus, in 1926 when he was seventeen, he was graduated from high school a second time.

His Grandmother Williamson provided funds for him to attend the University of Georgia in 1926, 1927, and 1928, preparing to obtain a law degree with a view toward being an attorney. At the University, his warm, engaging personality served him well. He made friends quickly and easily, as he would all his life, and he was a member of Lambda Chi Alpha Fraternity and Sigma Delta Kappa Fraternity.

The Great Depression intervened, however, and by 1929 he left the University of Georgia in Athens, never to return. He went home to the family farm where times were hard, and returned to a pursuit he knew well—he could still plow a straight furrow following behind a stubborn mule, but it was not easy to go from the classroom and social functions on a campus almost 150 miles to the northeast back to a Dodge County farm.

In later years, he would recall that his mule was so weak from lack of food that he would have to "hoist" him up to keep him going. Apparently, if the mule lay down, he could not get up again without help. There were some who suspected that in later years Stuckey embellished his tales about his years on the farm and plowing his mule, but most of it was true. Times were indeed hard.

He took some solace in knowing that he had plenty of company at the beginning of the Great Depression. Nor were the dark days soon to end. The crash of 1929 was graphic evidence of the state of the country, and a real recovery was not to come until years later when World War II came along with its own set of problems.

Herbert Hoover had been inaugurated as the 31st president of the United States in 1929. "Black Friday" came on October 28 with the collapse of the New York Stock Exchange, and United States securities lost $26 billion in value. The country was immediately plunged into the depths of despair. Banks failed and fortunes were lost overnight. Countless men, unable to face the dark future, resorted to suicide. Although Amelia Earhart became the first woman to fly across the Atlantic, people were too immersed in trying to hold their lives together to acknowledge properly the real significance of the accomplishment.

In the midst of it all—perhaps in a desperate search for diversion—people were singing "Tiptoe Through the Tulips," "Georgia on My Mind," and "Walking My Baby Back Home."

Thus, at twenty years of age, Williamson Sylvester Stuckey must have felt that fate had dealt him a cruel blow. With his education interrupted, his prospects were bleak. It was just as well that he did not know it would be a dozen years before the country would begin to pull itself out of the Great Depression. Nevertheless, he assessed his options. And in the meantime he kept plowing his mule.

The first opportunity that opened to young Williamson Sylvester Stuckey would take him far from the rolling farmland he loved in Dodge County. In 1929 he took a job as a fruit inspector for the Department of Agriculture in the state of New York. His agricultural background helped to qualify him for this position. But he could not shake the Dodge County soil out of his boots, and soon returned home to the farm where he once again helped his father by plowing and other farm chores.

Although no one is certain exactly when it actually occurred, it was about this time that he was no longer known as "Sylvester" Stuckey. He became "Stuckey," and this name was to remain throughout his life. His business associates, friends, family, and even his wife always referred to him as "Stuckey."

As opportunities presented themselves, Stuckey did odd jobs, and for a time traveled for the Balfour Company, selling high school rings to members of graduating classes during the spring months, and returning to the farm in the fall. It is also reported that at one time Stuckey had a stint of working in the wheat fields of Kansas, but no one knows exactly when this was.

Always enterprising, even in those difficult days, he invented a computing scale for quickly figuring the cost of gasoline sold by filling station operators, and he endeavored to sell it. However, as he told a writer on the *Times-Journal Spotlight* in Eastman, "They'd rather figure it out in their heads, and they wouldn't buy the thing." Nevertheless, the fact that he invented the product indicated that his entrepreneurial inclination was developing. If one project or idea was not successful, he simply moved on to something else. That "something else" proved to be what would lead him eventually to his highly successful business enterprises.

By 1930 the Depression was deepening. Times were even harder. Hoboes who rode the rails into Dodge County were combing the countryside, asking for handouts of food. Money was short. No one knew when or how it would end. And when people sang, "Brother, Can You Spare a Dime?," they were not being facetious. Housewives, sympathizing with the hoboes' plight, would sometimes share with the grateful men scraps of food from their kitchen or pones of cornbread baked for their husbands' hunting dogs. Or they would simply invite the hoboes to eat their fill from the backyard scuppernong vines or to help themselves from the loaded pear trees. No one worried about security in those desperate days, and doors were never locked.

Almost in desperation, Stuckey asked a family friend, Fred E. Bennett, Sr., a feed, seed and fertilizer dealer in Eastman, "to give me a job if you have ANYTHING I can do." Bennett, as the story goes, said, "Well, I don't have a job for you, but how about traveling around and buying up pecans for me? I'll try to find a market and we'll ship them." "Boy, I jumped at the chance," Stuckey said.

Chapter 3

$35 AND HE'S ON HIS WAY

The only requirement for Stuckey to enter the pecan buying market was that he start out with some cash of his own, and this was something he simply did not have. Once again, Grandmother Williamson came to his rescue, lending him $35. She also asked him if he knew one variety of pecan from another, and he did not. She assembled paper bags with samples of different pecans in them, and carefully labelled them Stuart, Schley, etc.

Stuckey was in business. He admitted that he referred privately many times in the beginning to those paper bag samples, but he was a quick learner. And soon the samples were no longer needed. "I did try to hide my ignorance, though, and tried not to let a farmer see me looking in my bags," Stuckey recalled in an interview years later.

It was not an easy job, by any means, but it was a job. "During pecan season, we traveled day and night, buying from a handful of pecans at the time to a large quantity," he said. During this time he had valuable help from John King, a black man who worked on the family farm. He joined Stuckey in his travels in search of pecans.

King recalled in an interview, "During them days we wouldn't have nothing to eat at dinner time and Mr. Stuckey would tell me to go on and eat some more of them pecans."

The Model A Ford Stuckey drove was not in good condition, and John frequently patched the tube of a tire when they had a flat, which sometimes was as many as a dozen times a day. After a year, Stuckey cited some progress: "John and I bought a two-wheel trailer the next year, and we could then put the pecans somewhere besides in the back of the Ford." (John King was later to work for Stuckey's and eventually would own a store. Stuckey never forgot his friends.)

During the first two years, Bennett bought almost all the nuts brought in by the young buyer, and they were shipped to outside markets. Stuckey was grateful for his profit of one cent per pound on the sales.

Although Stuckey was not making a great deal of money, his sales of pecans were beginning to increase. It was a beginning. He was gradually expanding his territory, reaching out to buy pecans in an ever widening area around Eastman. But he was also pursuing other interests, as he would do all his life.

He was, in fact, doing well enough financially to wed a local belle, Ethel Mullis, on December 24, 1931, in Dodge County. They became husband and wife in a ceremony at the home of Ethel's brother, G. Dewey Mullis, in Eastman. The white Victorian cottage is still standing today.

Ethel, a member of a large and well-known Dodge County family, was born April 15, 1909, in Dodge County, the daughter of Charles N. Mullis (February 2, 1872—November 26, 1944) who was sheriff of Dodge County for sixteen years, and Mary Etta Tripp Mullis (April 17, 1876—May 27, 1948.) Thus began a lifetime partnership, with Ethel supporting and assisting him in his business ventures through the years.

Ethel Mullis Stuckey's family background was similar in many ways to that of her husband. While five Stuckey brothers settled in Dodge County, only three Mullis brothers came, but they brought with them two first cousins. According to the *History of Dodge County* by Mrs. Wilton Philip Cobb, the three brothers were C.N., Joel and Cornelius Mullis, and the cousins were Alfred and "Old Man Charlie." The dates of their coming to Dodge County are not known. C.N. Mullis was Ethel's grandfather, and her father was C.N. Mullis, Jr. He and Mary Etta Tripp Mullis had eleven children: Ethel, Birdie, Pearl, George, Lewis, Newt, Mary Lizzie, Hazel, Orene, Ruth and Sara. Stuckey and his new wife set up housekeeping with Grandmother Williamson on the family farm, where they would remain until 1942 when they moved into Eastman.

After she married Stuckey, Ethel worked as a secretary for two County School Superintendents. She worked for both Moses Tunnell and W.C. Rozier in their terms of office. She also owned a beauty shop in Eastman as an investment. She did not operate the shop, nor was she a beautician. For her day, she was an enterprising woman.

Stuckey did not believe in "putting all his eggs in one basket," and this was a philosophy he followed throughout his life, even after the candy business had surpassed all his expectations. A family friend, Mrs. Elizabeth Harrell, remembers that when Stuckey and Ethel were married, he was selling wood to make a living in addition to pecans. He was always diversified and he always kept his options open. This may have been a hard-learned lesson of the Depression years, or it may have been his own good business instincts. During this period, he also operated a cross-tie business in 1933 and 1934. Also in 1933 he began buying pecans for himself and selling them directly to processors.

That first $35 which his grandmother lent Stuckey has become an oft-repeated part of the Stuckey legend. In truth, however, the $35 was loaned to him over and over again, in fact, every morning for awhile. Thus, it was a sort of revolving fund. He would pay it back every night and borrow it again the next day, just to keep himself going. To put it in perspective, however, it is important to remember that $35 in those days represented a far larger amount of money than it does today.

Another oft-repeated story about this period involves his unique relationship with a local bank, the Citizens Clearing

Bank. Eventually, the $35 advance was not enough to cover his expenses as he began to purchase larger amounts of pecans. He would make the purchases late in the day, paying for them by check, then get up early the next morning to get to the bank to deposit enough money to cover the checks written the previous day. The banking hours in those days were 6 a.m. to late afternoon, so it was a safe arrangement for him. Amazingly, he never had a check to bounce.

In an interview, Stuckey is reported to have said, "If I used my money too early in the day, I'd wait until the banks closed and start writing checks. Then I'd sell the pecans at night and be waiting on the doorstep when the bank opened the next morning."

Claude Alexander Ragan, a partner in the Citizens Clearing Bank, became his good friend and mentor. In later years, Stuckey would say, "If there hadn't been a Claude Ragan, there would never have been a Stuckey's."

According to Ragan's widow, Mrs. Verna Lee Ragan of Eastman, Stuckey could not get credit anywhere but at her husband's bank. He first borrowed $200—then six hundred—and in 1934 he was granted a loan of $2,000. By the fall of 1936, he needed still more funds, and applied for a $20,000 loan. Because the small private bank had only a limited amount of money to lend, it simply could not supply the needs of the growing Stuckey pecan wholesale business. Stuckey always credited Ragan with providing him with an entry into the Macon financial world, enabling him to borrow money for future growth at a larger bank in Macon. By 1936 he was handling approximately $150,000 worth of pecan sales annually. Ragan died in 1937, but throughout his life, Stuckey never forgot his friend and mentor, and he always acknowledged his indebtedness to the man. He maintained contact and friendship with Mrs. Ragan, and for a number of years she worked for Stuckey's.

Mrs. Ragan recalls that Stuckey told her an interesting story from his youth. "He said that when he was a boy he would come to town and walk by and admire the big white Victorian home on the corner which would later become his home. He thought it was the prettiest house he had ever seen." He never lost his admiration for that home, and eventually he would purchase it in the mid-1940s. The home is still owned today by the Stuckey family.

Another mentor, M.M. Monroe of Waycross, was also credited with lending money to Stuckey. Billy Stuckey recalls hearing his father say that Mr. Monroe lent him money at 2 percent per month, a lot for that time, but Stuckey considered him his good friend.

In an interview many years later, Stuckey reminisced, "It was tough going at first (the wholesale pecan business). We would work so hard and so late loading cars, we'd just go to sleep on top of the bags." In those early days, there was absolutely no inkling that this hardworking young man had the "magic touch" that would catapult him into a multi-million dollar business, based on the little valued pecan.

For the country there finally was light at the end of the tunnel, however feeble its glimmer. A man called Franklin Delano Roosevelt was elected President of the United States in the fall of 1932 in a landslide victory over Herbert Hoover. He was inaugurated as the 32nd president in 1933. Badly frightened and extremely worried, people in Dodge County and all over the country gathered in little knots in the homes of those fortunate enough to have a newfangled invention called a radio, to hear the new president's inaugural address. In strong, melodic tones, he told his captive audience, "The only thing we have to fear is fear itself." And the desperate listeners clung to his every word and dared to believe that it might be true.

The new president, viewed immediately as something of a Messiah, plunged into action and quickly announced a banking holiday, effectively ending the plague of the banking crisis. Then, without delay, Roosevelt instituted his New Deal which involved, in effect, the use of the authority of government as an organized form of self-help for all classes, groups, and sections of the country. Such acronyms as WPA

(Works Progress Administration) and CCC (Civilian Conservation Corps) became household words offering rays of hope to the impoverished land. In 1935, Roosevelt signed the Social Security Act, a revolutionary idea for beleaguered citizens who were too busy trying to get through one day at the time to give thought to their future welfare. Even so, there was still a long way to go before prosperity would return.

Stuckey's father, William Ira, re-married on September 14, 1928 in Chauncey to Wilma Lowe (born September 28, 1901). In the wedding announcement in the Dodge County newspaper, William Ira was described as a "prosperous farmer of Eastman, Route Seven." During this period, as far as is known, however, there was no contact between father and son.

The son of William Ira and Wilma Lowe Stuckey was born on November 11, 1933, in Dodge County. They named him William Frank Stuckey. On May 25, 1935, Stuckey's son, Williamson Sylvester Stuckey, Jr., was born. Young Billy gave Stuckey another good reason to work even harder than before. The young family continued to live on the Williamson farm. Thus, William Frank Stuckey, Stuckey's half-brother, was twenty-four years younger than Stuckey and closer in age to Stuckey's son, Williamson Sylvester Stuckey, Jr., than to Stuckey himself.

Meanwhile, Stuckey was concentrating on what he thought was the major part of his business—buying and shipping pecans. By 1935 he had begun his advertising which would become the foundation of his marketing in later years. He put out signs to attract those passing through Eastman to his pecan operation located in a nondescript building.

Throughout this period, Ethel Stuckey worked with her husband in the warehouse, helped out with record keeping and whatever tasks that were needed. At the time that Billy was born, the Stuckeys were still living in the country in the old farmhouse with Grandmother Williamson. The house had no modern conveniences, typical of rural Georgia farmhouses of the period.

Early in the decade of the 1940s, Stuckey moved his young family from the country to Eastman, where he bought a three-story white frame house on Griffin Street. This house, as remembered by Ethel's niece, Jane Benton Wingate, was a "beautiful home with hardwood floors." Grandmother Williamson went along with them when they moved to town, and she would live with the family as a sort of resident matriarch until her death.

The country trusted FDR so much that he was reelected for a second term in 1936, with yet another landslide. Slowly the New Deal's programs were beginning to work, and little by little the economy was improving.

Scant attention was paid in Dodge County to the reported international gossip about King Edward VIII's relationship with Mrs. Wallace Simpson, but a bit later when the king abdicated and announced his intention to marry "the woman I love" and became the Duke of Windsor, the whole world's attention was captured.

Popular songs of the day included "Flat Foot Floogie with a Floy Floy," and "A Tisket, a Tasket," and the Lambeth Walk was the fashionable dance of the day. A little girl with golden curls danced her way into the hearts of everyone. Most towns by then had a movie house, and crowds of all ages flocked to see the country's new idol, Shirley Temple, in "The Littlest Colonel" and "Little Miss Marker." And the whole country, and much of the world, agonized over the disappearance of Amelia Earhart on her flight in the Pacific in 1937.

Chapter 4

IN THE BEGINNING THERE WAS A ROADSIDE STAND

In 1936 an unrecognized but historic event occurred. Stuckey opened a roadside stand for the sale of pecans. The occasion might well have been paraphrased, "In the beginning there was a roadside stand."

In later years, Stuckey sometimes referred to the stand as a "shack." It was a board structure, made of slabs, with a sloped-back roof, indistinguishable from countless others that dotted the nation's highways then, with everything from cane juice and syrup to homemade quilts for sale. The stand was in reality a trial balloon, a test without much of a capital investment, simply to see if the idea would work.

To vacation-bound tourists who passed the stand on the outskirts of Eastman, Georgia, it certainly could not have looked like the forerunner of a multi-million dollar enterprise—a business whose blue-roofed stores became America's roadside standard of excellence in motoring services, candy, snacks, and souvenirs.

Indeed, while there were no special qualities to distinguish the stand from countless others, there was something very out-of-the-ordinary about the strapping, six-foot-four-inch Georgian whose name was emblazoned across the front—a fellow by the name of W.S. Stuckey. In the words of an

Eastman crony, "Stuckey's got the gumption of three ordinary men. Like as not he could make a success out of raisin' mice and sellin' them to ladies' bridge clubs for prizes."

The legendary story goes that one day when the roadside stand was already going rather well, Stuckey had a brainstorm. "Why not add some candy to our merchandise?" So he rushed home, interrupted one of Ethel's bridge games, and led her to the kitchen to whip up a batch of pralines. (This was typical of Stuckey—his ideas or brainstorms were usually followed by immediate action. But he was just as quick to drop an unsuccessful effort.)

In later years, Ethel Stuckey would recall that she really did not know how to make candy, but she muddled through, and turned out the first batch of Stuckey's candy. Although completely unrecognized at the time, it was a historical event. The pralines sold well and later Ethel became quite proficient at the art of candy making, expanding to include divinity and fudge. She would make batches of candy, and Stuckey would be waiting to deliver it to the stand. Thus was the inauspicious beginning of Stuckey's candy. He soon put up another sign near the one by the roadside: "Fresh Homemade Candy—Made Today." His belief in advertising, particularly with roadside billboards, was strong and effective.

The pralines began selling like hot-cakes, and divinity and fudge were close behind. Ethel Stuckey found herself spending a great deal of time in the kitchen, making several batches a day and having less time for bridge. As candy sales increased, Ethel enlisted her sisters, Hazel and Pearl, to help her with the candy-making, using a regular mixer, not even a utility-size, and they worked hard to turn out the candy the tourists were gobbling up.

Sylvia Rubin, Ethel's friend from the early days of her marriage, remembers going with Ethel to deliver pralines to the roadside stand when the Stuckeys were living at the old farmhouse. "Ethel was in a bridge club, and they invited me to play, probably to fill in, then I was invited to join the club." She remembers bridge games being interrupted when Ethel would have to take candy out to the store on Hawkinsville Road. Mrs. Rubin also reminisces about being with Ethel when they would drive up to the local drug store, tooting the horn for curb service, and ordering a "dope" (what Coca-Cola was called in those days).

Mrs. Rubin spent a lot of time with the Stuckeys while her husband, Sol Rubin, was in service during World War II. He is now a dentist in Eastman. "We also ordered our groceries by telephone in those days," Mrs. Rubin recalls. Mrs. Rubin remembered that Stuckey and Ethel worked hard, but they liked to have fun and "party," too. Ethel would find a babysitter or park the children somewhere, and they would get together, pack picnic food, and go to Bembry's Mill near Hawkinsville. "We'd play penny poker and have so much fun," she said.

Stuckey always gave Ethel full credit for her work and said, "Ethel helped me all the time, even at the first downtown store. She could beat me buying pecans any day in the week."

Whatever Stuckey did, working or playing, he did it with all his heart, putting everything he had into it. But he was never a workaholic.

When the winter's business proved encouraging, Stuckey decided to sell the roadside stand to a farmer for use as a hen house, demonstrating the frugality for which he was known. He then built a bona fide store, probably using capital that included what he made from the sale of the roadside stand. This store grossed between $25,000 and $30,000. Stuckey was on his way. But the business was not an instant, overwhelming success.

Along about this time, a man by the name of Boots Fluellen started working for Stuckey. He and Stuckey had known each other all their lives. Boots was assigned to duties that were all-purpose—in later years he would serve as a chauffeur for Stuckey and his family, but in the beginning he simply did what needed to be done, working around the office, running errands, or lending a hand in Ethel's kitchen. Boots was a legendary character, and everyone who ever knew Stuckey has an amusing story or a fond memory about Boots. His loyalty to Stuckey was something of a legend.

In 1939 Stuckey branched out even further by opening a second store in nearby Unadilla, Georgia on the well-travelled U.S. 41. The manager Stuckey hired for the Unadilla store had been working at a grocery store for $18 a week. Stuckey hired him for $12 a week, but furnished him with an apartment, water, lights and heat. This is the first known example of his practice of rewarding employees with fringe benefits and opportunities rather than large salaries. In 1940 he transferred operations in Eastman to a station south of Eastman, the same location which would become the mainstay of his vast operations in later years.

His daughter, Lynda, joined the family on December 6, 1940. The Stuckey family was still living in the old farmhouse in the country, but by now Stuckey and Ethel had renovated and updated it to include some modern conveniences and carpeting.

Jane Benton Wingate, Ethel's niece, was a young girl of seven when Billy was born in 1935. She spent a lot of time with Ethel and Stuckey, helping with chores and babysitting. She felt fortunate to receive 50 cents per week for her efforts. Jane was older by the time Lynda was born, and she baby-sat more with Lynda than Billy, however.

Stuckey took great pride in his son and daughter. He liked to have them near him and took them along with him to the office often. In Eastman, his son was known as "Billy," and to this day this is how he is known to family and home folks; otherwise, he is Bill Stuckey, Jr. (Because this work is family oriented, he is referred to as "Billy" here.)

One of Billy's earliest memories, not surprisingly, has to do with pecans. He was four years old or so when he first remembers going to his father's business, a wholesale pecan establishment on the main street in Eastman. "I used to go and play on the piles of pecans and spend a lot of time down there. I remember when the first store was being built for a very childlike reason. I stuck a nail in my foot at the construction site—things like that have a way of making you remember them."

At the time when Billy can first remember, his father was struggling to establish the pecan wholesale and candy businesses, as well as trying out various other enterprises. "As I look back, I don't think Dad ever had any planned design for his business, but he had an entrepreneurial spirit, and if he had not succeeded in the candy business, he would have succeeded at something else."

At various times in his life Stuckey had a furniture business, a funeral home in Ellaville, Chrysler and Dodge-Plymouth dealerships in Eastman, a black night club in Eastman, and a tractor dealership, and sold railroad crossties and stick candy during the war. His land acquisitions, timber and farming interests, came later on. At one time in the 1950s, he owned oil wells in Texas. He was diversified.

In his youth, Billy spent much time riding with his father over farm and timber land. Later, when old enough, Lynda also went on such jaunts with her father. "Every minute he could spare, he was out looking at his land," Billy recalled. "He was trying to quit smoking during these years, and he started chewing tobacco on these trips. He would not chew tobacco in the office or plant. He would spit tobacco juice all over the car and everywhere. He really loved the country—he loved Dodge County."

Business continued to grow so well that Stuckey opened a third store, in Folkston, Georgia, near the Florida state line, on one of the main arteries for tourists.

By the time Lynda was born, the business was beginning to achieve a measure of success, probably beyond Stuckey's expectations. He could not know that the dark days of World War II lay ahead. Billy was five years old when his sister was born. Despite the difference in their ages, the brother and sister formed a close bond. Although they would be separated by their schooling as teenagers, they have remained close throughout their lives. The two share their father's love for Eastman and Dodge County.

One summer day when Mrs. Rubin drove up to the Stuckey home, their first one in town, Lynda was playing in the front yard, making mud pies and decorating them with boysenberries. When she asked Lynda what she was doing, she replied, "I's making money." Like father, like daughter.

Stuckey's grandmother, Cora Williamson, was very influential in his life, his son said. "His mother died when he was young, and he and his father did not get along. I never met my Grandfather Stuckey but one time—on a street in Eastman—he spoke to me and asked who I was, but I am sure he already knew."

Billy remembers, his Great Grandmother Williamson's living in their home. "I used to sleep with her at night," he recalls. "My Grandfather Williamson had already passed away. When I was born, my parents were living with Grandmother Williamson."

Although the country was concerned about the conditions in Europe and the plight of England as Germany waged war, it was considered to be "their affair and not ours." Indeed Europe seemed a great distance from these shores, and isolationism was popular. Still the United States Office of Price Administration (OPA) was established, a freeze on steel prices was initiated, and rubber rationing began, all as precautionary measures.

Despite all of this, no one was really prepared for an event which occurred in 1941, the far-reaching effects of which would be felt for years to come, in Dodge County, across the country, and around the world. On December 7, 1941, the Japanese attacked Pearl Harbor, and World War II began. Life for Stuckey and for the whole country would never be the same again.

Chapter 5

NO SUGAR, NO GAS, NO TIRES, NO TOURISTS

With the dawning of 1942 came the full realization that the country was indeed at war. Men drafted for one year's service before the war began who had been singing, "I'll Be Back In A Year, Little Darling," changed their tune. No one knew how many years the fighting men would be away, nor indeed whether they would ever return. It soon became evident that this was not to be a short-lived conflict.

Wheels began turning very quickly to institute a new policy of austerity for all the citizens of the country in support of the defense effort, and much of this was achieved by a rationing system. Although it took a few months to organize the system and make it operational, by the spring of 1942, rationing was fully instituted. In March 1942, 190 million copies of War Ration Book One, containing 28 stamps for sugar, coffee and shoes, were printed. By mid-1942 the government had halted production of such items as bicycles, wagons, skates, and even balloons. Many other drastic changes occurred, and lifestyles were vastly different almost immediately. All eligible males were drafted and went away to serve their country. Most young men, as soon as high school diplomas were received, quickly answered Uncle Sam's call. As time went on, men with families were also being drafted. Women who had never handled business matters were suddenly in charge of the family, with husbands away at war, and many entered the work force in defense plants and as civilian employees at military bases. The construction business quickly ground to a halt because building materials were no longer available for civilian purposes. Automobile manufacturers did not put out any new models for the war's duration. Many industries converted to defense plants. Victory gardens, large and small, even handkerchief-sized plots located in corners of vacant lots downtown, were cultivated for growing vegetables, to help the country's food supply. Civilians invested heavily in United States Savings Bonds, and children bought savings stamps with their earnings and allowances, holding onto them until they had enough to buy bonds. Georgia's coastal cities had blackouts or brownouts, and practice air raids came fairly often even for inland towns and cities. Civilians willingly served as air raid wardens.

The formalities of wedding etiquette took a back seat to Uncle Sam, and countless weddings took place on short notice, whenever the groom-serviceman could get a furlough or leave. Families dreaded those telegrams, all too common, which began, "The War Department regrets to inform you that..." The country was united in a great wave of patriotism, and people were willing to make whatever sacrifices it took to win the war. Frightening headlines such as "Rommel Launches New Offensive" and "Japanese Occupy Bataan" shocked readers of morning newspapers. Times were far from normal.

Stuckey must have pondered, however briefly, the hand that had been dealt to him, just as his hard work of almost a decade was beginning to pay off, and he was expanding his stores. In fact, a lesser man might easily have been excused had he abandoned his dream, folded his tents and silently stolen away to some other endeavor. But he was not an ordinary man and not one to spend much time bemoaning his fate—he simply looked at his options and decided to make the best of it.

Still, the question of how to get sugar for candy-making must have been monumental. There was no way to get around the fact that in order to make candy, he had to have sugar. And to have a successful candy business, he had to have customers. The tourist trade dried up—no one could get enough gasoline and automobile tires to travel very far. Besides, the pre-war family car had to be coddled so it would last until the war was over.

In 1943 President Roosevelt froze wages, salaries, and prices to forestall inflation, and a pay-as-you-go income tax system was instituted. Juke boxes across the country were playing "Mairzy Doats," "Comin' in on a Wing and a Prayer," and "When the Lights Go On Again All Over the World." A new dance called the jitterbug was taking the country by storm.

Each of Stuckey's stores made its own candy, and in the new Folkston store, there was a small supply of sugar, 1,000 to 1,500 pounds or so. Stuckey said in an interview in later years, "The St. Mary's River is down on the Georgia-Florida line, and up and down the river they had this lot of bootleggers. One night right after Pearl Harbor, someone (believed to be a bootlegger) broke into this store, stole the sugar, and set the building on fire." Thus, the Folkston store was an early, though indirect, casualty of the war.

Due to the creative management of its founder, the Stuckey store in Eastman was able to remain open throughout the war. Some attributed this feat entirely to Stuckey's strong sense of survival, another lesson he learned well during the hard Depression years which shaped his life.

"The only way we could afford to keep it (the Eastman store) open was because I was able to get one or two of the bus drivers to make it a regular stop. They would tell the other bus drivers, so that every bus that came along would stop at the store. That's the only thing that kept us in business. We would find them cigarettes, shotgun shells, shoe stamps, and meat stamps, and just give them to the drivers, because they were stopping at the store," Stuckey said in an interview.

Once the war was really under way, it was "no sugar, no gas, no tires, no tourists," as Stuckey described the situation. "Naturally, if we stayed in business we were forced to reduce expenses to a bare minimum. We closed some stations and changed our plans," he commented wryly.

People in Eastman watched the almost constant parade of Army convoys which passed through town on their way to various camps in Georgia. Stuckey, however, saw the presence of the Army jeeps and trucks as an opportunity, and the germ of an idea began to form, an idea which would be his means of surviving the war years.

"The ration board limited us people who made candy at that time to certain amounts of sugar, depending on what we had used in the past. But if you sold to the Army, or any of the armed forces, they would give you replacement sugar, so we were seeking that type of business," Stuckey said in an interview, recalling the details of his efforts to build the military business. "I had nerve enough to go to Atlanta to see if I could find some boxes, where I was able to talk this gentleman in the box business into giving me a small supply. He had to ration his boxes out, because he didn't have enough."

Before the war, Stuckey had sold pecans and candies in bags only. It was doing business with the military that prompted him to convert to attractive candy boxes. The changeover was good for business, Stuckey noted. "The attractively-boxed items sold much better, and I suppose, tasted better to the customer," he remarked.

Stuckey hired a salesman who sold 1,000 boxes of candy on his first trip to Camp Stewart near Savannah. "That," Stuckey exclaimed, "set us on fire. I had a kind of a warehouse that I was using at the time for buying and selling wholesale pecans. I partitioned it off and made rooms, concreted the floor, and made a little candy kitchen back there. I had Coleman burners and eight- and ten-quart boilers, and we would cook that divinity, fudge, pralines, and brittle. The building was only 240 square feet, but it served the purpose."

The salesman went to several other Army camps, and was able to get orders nearly everywhere he went. He built his business up to the point where Stuckey hired a professional candy maker about 1943 or 1944. By that time they were servicing Army camps in several Southern states. The Stuckey products became so famous and popular among servicemen throughout the nation that the plant in Eastman operated three shifts, day and night. Because his employees in the plant were primarily from Eastman, this boosted the local economy.

The large volume of business he was experiencing with the military also led Stuckey to expand his business. But the problem of obtaining sugar still hung over him. He bought a small candy plant in Jacksonville, Florida, in order to get a larger quota of sugar. "But I had to operate it in Jacksonville because the sugar was designated for that area, and the customers were there. I fudged on the government a little bit about how much sugar went into each pound of candy." The plant produced several types of candy.

Most of the Stuckey business remained with the military, but gradually the company began to acquire more and more patronage from private business. At that time Stuckey's Candy sold for 55 cents per pound or two pounds for $1.

Stuckey made some candy sales to Rich's (one of the largest department stores in the South) in Atlanta. He always kept his ears open, and heard about a department store candy convention that would be held in Atlanta, attended by buyers from many department stores. This was a golden opportunity for sales contacts, and he managed to attend. They asked him how much production he could supply—but he did not have enough sugar to produce very much. "I got out and found me a place where I could buy some black market sugar," Stuckey declared.

"At that time I was getting most of my sugar out of Miami. I hired a long, tall black named Joe Serpent, and I bought a big, big old cavalry engine truck, and we would go down and bring back about 20,000 pounds of sugar at a time. When we would come through the state line, we would have to stop for inspection.

"They would say, 'What you got there?'

And he would say, 'Sugar.'

They would ask, 'Who is it for?'

He would say, 'Mr. Stuckey.'

And they would say, 'Go ahead.'"

Stuckey knew the inspector. His store in Folkston was right across the street. This served him well.

In an interview, Stuckey continued, "Along about then, when they issued you sugar, they gave it to you in the form of a check, which you deposited in the bank just like you did money. When you went to a wholesale grocer to buy sugar, you would write a check for the amount you needed. I had bought 50,000 pounds from a man named Joe Howard in Miami. He came up here looking for me; that was my first contact. We got together on twelve cents per pound, by the month. In other words, I was to pay him twelve cents per pound, and he was going to mail me a check; then whatever I could buy the sugar for would be twelve cents plus that price."

Stuckey recalled that one day two FBI agents came to Eastman and questioned him and his drivers. The agents were told the truth about the sugar and left. Eventually, the FBI broke up the Florida black market sugar ring, but left Stuckey alone. One agent is said to have summed up the attitude of the FBI toward Stuckey succinctly: "We know he's not black market, and we know he is not selling sugar to bootleggers. We know he's making candy out of it, and therefore we don't even bother."

As a result, Stuckey was later to ponder the totally unexpected gift which came to him out of the FBI investigation. "What had happened," Stuckey continued, "is that I bought the sugar checks from Jim Howard in Miami and gave him two checks for $3,000 each, one payable the first of the month and the other payable the first of the next month.

They had planted one of the FBI men in the candy plant in Miami as a bookkeeper or office worker.

"The agreement was that I would mail Jim Howard the two checks and he would mail me a check for 50,000 pounds of sugar. I got the sugar check before I mailed the money check, so when my money check arrived there with my name on the outside, the agent just picked it up, and they made a case against Jim Howard." The two checks sent by Stuckey to Howard were placed in a government file and never cashed. "You might say that I got 50,000 pounds of sugar at a record price," Stuckey recalled.

Meanwhile, the war went on, both in Europe and the Pacific. When word of D-Day came on June 6, 1944, the country held its breath and prayed for the brave men on more than 700 ships and 4,000 landing craft who invaded the European continent via Normandy. Many "regret to inform you" messages went to families after this invasion, and also later that year when the Battle of the Bulge in the Ardennes took place.

Billy Stuckey remembers a story which illustrates his father's inventiveness and creativity. This story was admittedly hushed up by the family for years. "During the war candy was scarce and in great demand—but you couldn't get sugar and you also couldn't get exotic things like coconut. So Dad got the idea of using his stick-candy factory in Jacksonville to help him out. He had stocked coconut flavoring there to use in making stick candy, so he added that to corn shucks from his farms, which he ground up to look like coconut. And he made a lot of money selling coconut candy sticks! I don't guess anyone suffered from eating corn shucks in stick candy."

Ethel Mullis Stuckey has been described as "the glue which held the Stuckey family together." She worked very closely with her husband in the early years, and she was involved in the important planning and decision-making. She was the co-founder of Stuckey's Inc., and later held the title of vice president. Even in later years when Stuckey's had become quite successful, she continued to contribute to that success. Her role, from the very beginning, was very substantive and important to the progress and development of Stuckey's, Inc., and Stuckey relied heavily upon her judgment and input.

Ethel's candy-making provided the very foundation for the business. She was proud of her role with Stuckey's and took great pride in Stuckey's success. During these years, she did yeoman's work—in the warehouse, in the office, and wherever she was needed. She traveled for the business, and displayed a real talent for finding high quality pecans and purchasing them at good prices, all the while combining such work with her homemaking duties and her role as a mother. In later years, although she was less involved in the up-front operations of the business, she maintained a deep interest in Stuckey's, and always knew what was taking place.

Meanwhile, during the war years Billy and Lynda were growing up. At the beginning of the war, Billy was six years old. Lynda's earliest memories are from the mid to latter parts of the war years, although she was not then aware of the war.

One of her memories is the joy and excitement associated with her father's homecoming late each afternoon. Of this time, Lynda remembers, "Daddy's special name for me was 'Lou,' and he would come in from work and call out, 'Lou, where are you?' I would come running and he would open his arms, pick me up, walk around a bit and talk to me. Then he would take me on his knee and talk to me about my day. He was always interested in me and what I did. I remember especially his hands—he had such big, beautiful hands."

Lynda continued, "Another time I remember—he was already in the new office building, not the very first one, though—Daddy kept souvenirs from different companies in a big drawer of his desk. I would come in, open that drawer and see what kinds of toys and gimmicks that I could find to play with. I think he must have kept them there to entertain me. He always loved for me to go to the office with him, and Billy always went, too, when he was little. He kept loose change in his pencil box, and I would sometimes borrow a quarter or two and leave an I.O.U. This amused him very much."

Stuckey liked children and treated them with dignity. In later years he also enjoyed taking his grandchildren to the office with him. Most often, though, he would get busy, an important telephone call would come in, and his longtime secretary, Elva Lee Connell, would watch over the children and entertain them.

At times Stuckey could be a disciplinarian, but most of the time this was left to Ethel's discretion. "On occasion, he would punish us and even occasionally would spank us," Lynda recalls. "It worked, and when he spoke, I listened. He was so big, such a giant to a little girl, and I loved him so much, that I wanted to please him by obeying. As I look back, though, I can see that my mother made me do things on my father's word, so she became the bad guy. He may have been more strict with Billy than with me. I don't know, but I expect so. What I remember most is that all my life my father was always there when I needed him. I had a happy childhood in Eastman."

The whole country went into deep mourning over the unexpected death of Franklin Delano Roosevelt at Warm Springs, Georgia, on April 12, 1945. With victory so near, it seemed an unfair twist of fate that the man who had led the country out of the Great Depression, and through World War II to this point, did not live to experience V-E Day on May 8, less than a month later. Nor was he to enjoy the final victory of V-J Day in August. For twelve years FDR had been at the helm, and suddenly a little known man from Missouri, Harry S. Truman, was in the Oval Office as the 33rd President. A big question mark of uncertainty fell like a shadow over the country.

With the ending of the war, Stuckey looked about him and assessed his assets and his options. He and Ethel had a growing family to consider—Billy was now ten years old, and Lynda was almost five years old. He had a good profit base from the $150,000 worth of candy he had sold to the armed forces. The stage was set for a boom in the country's business, and Stuckey was not about to be left behind. He was ready to strike out and be a part of the big push forward.

Williamson Sylvester Stuckey had come through World War II, and for him the future looked bright. He had paid his dues. He was ready. He was a survivor.

Chapter 6

THE LITTLE ROADSIDE STAND GROWS UP

The same innate abilities, entrepreneurial skills, and tenacity which enabled Stuckey to survive the war years served him well in the postwar period. Although the war had ended, some rationing was to continue for several years until the country eased back into a state of normalcy. The rationing of sugar, in fact, continued until 1948. This did not deter Stuckey from re-opening the Unadilla and Folkston stations, however.

Through an intermediary company that specialized in swapping commodities, Stuckey traded everything from cottonseed meal to automobiles to nylon stockings for sugar and corn syrup for his candy making. The Stuckey Company, in fact, became one of the largest traders in the country, and at one point even swapped Tom's Candies in Atlanta 100,000 pounds of corn syrup for 60,000 pounds of sugar.

A friend noted that Stuckey's uncanny ability for trading may have been a key factor in the survival of his business during the difficult years of the war. It was said that he would trade absolutely anything for sugar. Rumor even had it that he would swap fish guts for sugar if someone had sugar and wanted fish guts.

It was all a necessary part of building business and allocating resources in a postwar economy. And Stuckey did not intend to be left behind. The country was slowly returning to normal under President Truman's leadership.

"When they lifted the rationing on sugar, I closed the candy plant in Jacksonville. Of course we were expanding along as fast as we could, and I was also buying pecans during all those years, along with the other businesses," Stuckey said in an interview.

The "other businesses" included Stuckey's venture into construction, when this field opened up after the war. He built new stores as needed, and he also began to build houses around Eastman. While this was not a business which he would pursue very long, it did bring an Eastman man back home to serve as Stuckey's foreman of construction, thus beginning a long and profitable business association and friendship.

Russell D. Franklin, a native of Eastman, whom Stuckey had known during his youth, had been in Mississippi in the construction business for some years. He returned to Eastman toward the end of the war, and Stuckey contracted with him to build his station in Unadilla. Soon after the war ended, Franklin became a full-time employee of Stuckey's, handling the construction of new stations for the business. Franklin also rebuilt the burned-out Folkston station. It was about this time that Franklin created a new design for Stuckey stores, featuring steep roofs painted blue, making the buildings highly visible. This basic design, with some variations, became the standard one used for the stores throughout the country. Previously, the roofs had been flat. This standardization, providing instant recognition of a Stuckey Pecan Shoppe wherever located, was an important marketing tool.

Franklin's skills and experience in construction, as a contractor, businessman and administrator were put to good use in the candy business. In the early years, Franklin traveled a great deal for Stuckey's, doing location work for stores, contacting Chambers of Commerce and bankers, making preliminary arrangements. Before construction would begin, he would buy all the building materials, and then construction crews would come in from Eastman to begin construction. "We prided ourselves on being able to build and open a store in six weeks," said Franklin. "This was something we could do because we were streamlined. We had a standard plan."

Meanwhile, the country was gradually easing many of the restrictions and austerity which had been necessary to win the war. More than a million veterans were enrolled in college under the GI Bill. It was common to see returned veterans wearing parts of their military uniforms on college campuses— there either had not been enough time or sufficient money, or both, to outfit themselves in civilian clothes. And they were in a hurry to get on with their lives and make up for the lost years. Popular songs of the early postwar period included "Zip-A-Dee-Do-Dah," "Ole Buttermilk Sky" and "Doin' What Comes Natcherly."

The United States Congress passed the Marshall Plan calling for $17 billion in aid to Europe. And in 1948 Harry S. Truman, who had been serving the unexpired term of Roosevelt, was elected president, despite dire predictions that he would lose.

Stuckey's belief in diversity remained, and in addition to construction, he had bought a furniture store, and was also farming. The burgeoning success of the candy business did not in any way detract him from his basic philosophy. The pecan business continued to grow and to become increasingly profitable, and Franklin joined him as his first executive of the Stuckey Company.

In recalling this period, Franklin explained, "In the beginning I probably did not have a title. I just went to work for Stuckey. He had an office and I had an office. I think it was later that I became executive vice president." The setting for Stuckey's was not an auspicious one. A little tin building housed the executive offices, the accounting office, and the candy plant in those early postwar days.

Two important events took place in 1947. Stuckey's was incorporated, and the first partnership store was opened with Franklin at Sunnyside, Georgia. Thus began the franchise system which would be the foundation of the Stuckey chain. After that, instead of an annual raise, Franklin would receive an interest in a store. In 1948 a station was opened in Richmond Hill, Georgia. Stuckey was also operating a furniture store in Alamo, Georgia.

"As I began to expand," Stuckey commented, "instead of giving a man a raise, I would let him have an interest in a store, maybe a quarter interest. He would never put up any money. I would put the money up for him."

Stuckey truly liked to see his friends, relatives, and employees prosper, and he opened new doors of opportunities many of them had never dreamed existed. This explains the oft-repeated story that "there are more Cadillacs in Eastman than in any other small town in Georgia." Stuckey's brought prosperity to Eastman, and citizens of Eastman rejoiced over Stuckey's success.

It is said that the Internal Revenue Service became interested in the unusual prosperity which abounded in Eastman, setting this small town apart from others in South Georgia. An IRS man is said to have come to town to investigate, but apparently was satisfied with the explanation that no other town in the region was the home of Stuckey's. Nothing further was heard.

"Eastman was real progressive, even back in the 1940s as compared to other towns in the area. City and county governments worked together," recalls Franklin. "I believe it was an intangible result of the presence of Stuckey's. Not only did this have an impact on the economy, but there were cultural and civic advantages. Stuckey's brought in a diversity of people who joined the core group of Eastman employees who worked for Stuckey's."

Stuckey decided that while candy was still his most popular item, he was also convinced that gasoline would run a close second if he made it available. Billy Stuckey recalls, "Dad went to Texaco and said, `Look, I'm beginning to get a lot of stores. Why don't we work out a deal?' So they worked out a deal where Dad would sell only Texaco at his stores, and they would give him 3-1/4 cents profit on every gallon of gas he sold. When you figure that the average store was pumping 40,000 gallons of gas a month, that gets into lots and lots of money. And Dad was really innovative this time. That money didn't go to the company; it went to him personally." As Stuckey grew more prosperous, his business empire expanded. At the same time, those around him also were prospering.

People had been deprived of the luxury of travel for pleasure during the long war years, and they were ready to make up for lost time. Travel was at an all-time high in the last few years of the 1940s and into the 1950s. Americans were ready to enjoy their freedom and prosperity, and Stuckey was ready to help them.

In the midst of the growing prosperity of his candy business, however, Stuckey was remembering well the lessons he learned during hard times. The Stuckey Motor Company opened July 1, 1949, on College Street in Eastman. Owned by Stuckey, it was operated by Buddy NeSmith. Stuckey was said always to have "his fingers in many pies." Ever the trader, though, he sold the motor company to Jimmy H. Barnes in May 1952. Barnes also purchased the Stuckey Tractor and Equipment Company.

The war, however, and its accompanying atrocities were remembered well. A new book, *The Diary of Anne Frank*, a young Jewish girl's personal account of her life in Nazi Germany, served as a graphic reminder. In 1948, Dwight D. Eisenhower published his book, *Crusade in Europe*, which chronicled his years as Supreme Commander of the Allied Expeditionary Forces in Europe—including the command of the Allied invasion.

During these years newspapers reported international events such as Chiang-kai-shek's resignation as president of China, and his removal to Formosa (later Taiwan), but such happenings seemed far away. Most people in the United States were ready to turn their attention to the long-neglected home front. Romantic songs such as "Some Enchanted Evening" and "I'm in Love with a Wonderful Guy" held sway.

The Southern highways—notably U.S. 17, 301, 41 and I were thronged with automobiles. Weary travelers were ready and willing to stop at Stuckey's stores to buy Texaco gasoline, freshly squeezed orange juice, and homemade candy—and Stuckey's idea of using highway billboards to advertise his products pulled people in by the thousands. No other stores were really competing with what Stuckey's offered. A Stuckey's stop was seen as a welcome respite from the monotony of the road. In his marketing techniques, Stuckey was far ahead of his time.

Billy Stuckey recalls, "Those red and yellow billboards saying five miles to Stuckey's, four miles to Stuckey's, three, two, one would drive people crazy, but they'd stop there anyway. My father would tell me that it was not the candy, but the billboards, that was the real secret of his success." Motorists would complain about the frequency of the signs' locations, but this did not keep them from reading the messages, stopping, and shopping at Stuckey's.

Sometimes, after Stuckey's had grown larger, Stuckey would even forget where a billboard was located. They had to be repaired constantly and replaced, too. Farmers tore them down and used the materials to build pig pens and patch their barns. And hunters practiced target shooting on them, using the "e" in the Stuckey name as a bullseye. Later, Stuckey's half-brother, Frank, took on the responsibility of the billboards, along with other marketing.

Stuckey had long ago worked out his ingenious method of selecting a good location, preferably on the outside of a curve going north on a well-traveled divided highway, for his stores. This basic practice never changed. He liked to have what he called management teams, ideally a husband and wife who were middle-aged. In exchange for start-up money, the managers would sign a contract by which they agreed to sell only Texaco gasoline and Stuckey's candy which he sold them from his own factory. Thus, he would recover his investment almost immediately.

As the business expanded, he did not forget his old friend, John King, his assistant and constant companion during his early days of traveling over the countryside in a Model A Ford to buy pecans. John, who now worked for Stuckey's, got an interest in a Stuckey's store, too. But he was no exception.

Men who worked in Stuckey's warehouses and machine shops, and women who worked "on the line" in the candy plant also owned interests in the stores. About these people, he said, "They thought I was the Poppa of them all, and I had their respect. Very seldom did we have to fire anybody."

Almost all his office employees owned interests in stores, too. Elva Lee Connell, who began working as his secretary in 1948, (continuing until his death) owned interests in three or four stores. At one time Boots Fluellen also had an interest in a store. The name of Boots Fluellen comes up almost automatically when friends, family, and acquaintances reminisce about Williamson Sylvester Stuckey. Boots figured prominently in Stuckey's everyday life, and he was his constant companion.

The close relationship and the respect that Stuckey and Boots had for each other was established early in their lives. It is doubtful that Boots ever had an official title. He was Stuckey's friend in the largest sense. Described by an acquaintance as "blacker than the blackest black," Boots was illiterate, but in everything except book learning, he was highly intelligent, extremely astute, and perceptive. It has been said that Boots knew Stuckey as well as, and perhaps better than, anyone.

"I don't ever remember Dad's being without Boots," Billy Stuckey says. In fact, he often suspected that his father loved Boots as though he were a member of the family. He recalls, "Boots drove Dad around the countryside. He taught me how to drive and took me on my first date. Mother worshipped the ground Boots walked on, too. He was always part of the family, and that's how he was treated."

Elva Lee Connell remembers, "Mrs. Stuckey would sometimes preempt Boots to work in her kitchen. One day she had him shelling peas when Mr. Stuckey came in. He commented, 'Boots, you are the highest paid pea sheller in town.'"

Elva Lee said, "Mr. Stuckey depended on and trusted Boots. He treated Boots extremely well."

She recalls that Boots would say that he knew how to get the "best steaks in Eastman." He would simply tell the butcher, "These steaks are for Mr. Stuckey."

Charles Eckles of Eastman, who worked as an accountant for Stuckey's for many years, and later in sales, recalled, "Stuckey showed the same respect for Boots that he had for me or anyone else, bankers or whatever. He treated everybody the same, and, therefore, people were loyal to him."

Elva Lee recalls that when she went to work for Stuckey in 1948 he had seven or eight stores, and that by the time of his death in 1977 there were 350. She remembers that Stuckey knew all of his people by name. He was like a good shepherd who knew his sheep. "He would go into the candy plant and hug them, call them by name, and listen to their problems. He had a real feeling for people and he liked to share his wealth. It was a part of his philosophy to find and keep good people. He had a very low turnover in employment, not because he paid high wages but because the employees liked him and felt a loyalty to him. And he gave them the opportunity to acquire an interest in a store if they wanted to."

In the beginning and later when Stuckey's had expanded tremendously, he paid impromptu visits to stores. And somehow he would manage to know—or find out ahead of time—the names of the people who worked there, not just the managers, but also those who pumped the gasoline. He had a phenomenal memory, and a gift for putting people at ease. People appreciated this quality and they never forgot that Stuckey was their friend.

It did not matter to Stuckey whether a person was a high school dropout or at the management level. He delighted in people's success when they received interests in Stuckey stores. Because of their association with Stuckey's, many people improved their financial condition and enjoyed more prosperity, and Stuckey enjoyed seeing this happen. It was not just those associated directly with Stuckey stores, but also such people as poor sharecroppers in Dodge County who worked on the farms and timberland he was accumulating.

Stuckey made a real effort to help his franchisees when he could, particularly during the early years. He encouraged them and wanted success for them. Sometimes if a franchisee was having difficulty and was discouraged, he would do all he could to provide encouragement and support, and on occasion he would simply buy out the interest.

Ethel Stuckey had a well deserved reputation as a gracious hostess on all occasions, and she was always prepared for extra guests at meals. She gave strong support to her husband in his business, and provided a stable and serene home life for him and the family. She considered it her responsibility to provide for him the atmosphere and setting he needed to succeed. She took this responsibility seriously, and all who knew her say that she carried out these duties in an excellent manner.

Stuckey was likely to invite whomever he happened to be meeting with in the morning to go home with him to the mid-day meal, or "dinner" as this main meal was called. Or he might run into a friend on the street and say, "Come on home to eat dinner with me."

Stuckey's big white Victorian home, with its wide porches and high-ceilinged rooms and spacious accommodations, located in the heart of Eastman, provided a hospitable setting for entertaining, whether for impromptu or invited guests. Ethel Stuckey's menus regularly included plenty of fresh vegetables, cooked the old fashioned southern way and frequently seasoned with a ham hock, fried chicken, beef roast or country ham, cornbread, hot biscuits, and desserts such as strawberry shortcake in season, many-layered chocolate or coconut cakes, and homemade peach ice cream. This was not company fare—such abundance graced Ethel's table day in and day out. Stuckey did not need to alert her that guests were coming. He simply brought them home, knowing that she would welcome them, and that plenty of food would be prepared. His preference throughout his life was for good Southern "down-home" food, and Ethel knew how to provide it.

Through the years a number of Ethel's relatives worked for Stuckey's, and some had interests in Stuckey's stores. These included her sisters Birdie Mullis Giddens, Pearl Mullis Landers, Hazel Mullis Benton, Orene Mullis Burns, Ruth Mullis Williams, Mary Lizzie Mullis Winburn, and her brothers Lewis Mullis, Dewey Mullis, and Newt Mullis. Many of her brothers-in-law also worked for Stuckey's. In addition, the relationships with Stuckey's extended to the next generation of Ethel's family (that is, the daughters and sons and in-laws of Ethel's sisters and brothers), many of whom are still involved today. They were employed in various capacities: as managers, as owners of stores, and others as office workers, and still others were employed with the Stuckey Timberland business.

The celebrated pecan log roll was an extremely popular candy. It required the use of a special packaging machine that was said to look like a "Rube Goldberg" nightmare. Other popular Eastman-produced candies were fudge, pecan brittle, chocolates, and pralines. Thousands of pounds of peanuts were processed in the plant's roasters annually and vacuum-packed in jars and cans. Several tons of cashews and pistachios were imported yearly from India.

By the time that Stuckey reached his 39th birthday, in 1948, he had qualified for membership in a prestigious association, the Young President's Organization. He was justly proud of achieving this signal honor. To be eligible for membership, a person must head a million-dollar company before reaching his 40th birthday. In those days, soon after World War II ended, this was a phenomenal accomplishment, carrying far greater significance than it would today.

On a personal note, Stuckey and Ethel made the decision to send Billy to a military school for his high school years. Lynda, still in grammar school, was at home in Eastman.

Four stations opened in 1949: in White Springs and Chiefland, Florida, in Petersburg, Virginia, and in Statesboro, Georgia. Following closely, in 1950 stations were opened in Yulee, Florida; Cleveland, Tennessee; LaFolette, Tennessee; Tallulah Falls, Georgia; and Rockwood, Tennessee. New stations were opened in 1951 in Acworth and Wrens, Georgia; Summerton, South Carolina; South Pittsburg, Tennessee; Toomsuba, Mississippi; and Smithfield, North Carolina. And in 1952 Stuckey's reached out to include new stations in Sanford and Fletcher, North Carolina; Smith Grove and Georgetown, Kentucky; Loxley, Alabama, and Dinwiddie, Virginia.

Suddenly the "little roadside stand" had grown up and was expanding. Stuckey stores had become the accepted standard of quality across the southeast. The Midas touch was working for Stuckey, and the road ahead looked bright.

Chapter 7

STUCKEY AND HIS FRIENDS

Williamson Sylvester Stuckey was a complex personality, and depending on who is telling the story, he is remembered in various ways, occasionally with outright contradictions.

Physically, he was, as many have described him, an imposing presence, a big, handsome man, six feet four-inches tall, weighing 200 pounds, with dark hair and eyes. He kept a deep suntan as a result of his love of the outdoors. Although not an athlete, he was active and kept himself slim and trim.

One trait that almost all of Stuckey's friends, business associates and family attribute to him is complete dependability and trustworthiness. "His word was his bond" or similar words are repeated over and over as these persons reminisce about their associations with Stuckey. This remark was frequently followed by, "You didn't need it in writing if you had a handshake from Stuckey." He is also remembered as being open-minded, up to a point, in his decision making. He would listen to various viewpoints, then make up his mind on an issue, and after that did not wish to discuss the matter further. Although easygoing, to a degree, he could act very decisively and quickly when the circumstances warranted it.

His work ethic was typical for a man who had experienced the dark days of the Great Depression. He worked hard, and expected the same dedication from his staff and all his employees. Today's 9 a.m. to 5 p.m. routine had no meaning for him—if there was work to do, one did it, and did not watch the clock.

On the other hand, Stuckey never seemed to be preoccupied with business—he had a lighthearted approach to life. He enjoyed living and loved the business, both the personal and the social aspects of it. As a friend described him, "Stuckey was a happy man."

The late W.T. (Duck) Moody, a Macon banker who was also a business associate and close friend of Stuckey, recalled an occasion that illustrated a trait of Stuckey's character. Moody, who enjoyed telling a good story, leaned back in his chair in his home, and turned his thoughts backward. Moody was vice president of the First National Bank in Macon, a bank that later became Trust Company Bank of Georgia, and today is SunTrust Bank.

"One morning Stuckey called me," Moody began, "and he said, 'Duck, whatever you are doing, quit and come on down here. I have got a proposition going, and I want you to take a look at it.' I went on down to Eastman, and he showed me a big home on a lake owned by a fellow who wanted to sell it. The property included 25 acres of land and a house and the lake, and he wanted $125,000 for it. I approved, thought it was a good deal, and Stuckey wrote out a check for it and got a deed to the property. Two days later the man's circumstances changed, and he wanted the property back. Stuckey had not yet recorded the deed. He thought it over, tore up the deed and got his check back. He said it wouldn't be right to keep the property. That's the kind of man he was."

Stuckey organized countless trips for various friends to accompany him to the Kentucky Derby, the World Series, and the legendary Georgia-Florida football game. He enjoyed an occasional game of golf with friends, as well as hunting and fishing. He owned a boat which he kept at St. Simons Island, and nothing pleased him more than to see people enjoying themselves, whether he participated or not.

"What he really enjoyed was people," Billy explained, "and whatever made his friends happy made him happy. He loved the social aspect connected with these activities. He enjoyed the crowd, the partying, and the people."

His good friends, the Herschel Palmers, enjoyed the Kentucky Derby, too, and they would assemble a group of people, with Stuckey supplying the tickets and Herschel Palmer providing the train car. The congenial group would really have a wonderful time at the Derby. This was an annual event to which they all looked forward.

Lynda recalled, "Daddy played at golf some, but he really would rather work. He simply enjoyed seeing his friends have a good time. He liked to take along friends like Hugh Gillis, Duck Moody, Herschel Palmer ... he really liked people."

Describing a typical trip to the Derby, Senator Hugh Gillis, Sr. of Soperton, recalled: "Some of our best times together were at the Kentucky Derby. Stuckey and Ethel loved to ride the train more than any other mode of travel. My wife and I, Herschel Palmer and his wife, Tillie, Stuckey and Ethel, six of us, would go on a private car which would be connected to a passenger train in Atlanta. We would drive to Atlanta, get on the car, and spend about three days together. We were real close friends, and we would enjoy the company so much.

"Ethel loved to play bridge and cards—the whole group did—and we would play cards going up on the train and coming home. Stuckey loved to play poker, but Ethel was really better at it than he was. She could almost tell what you had in your hand, and sometimes she would say, 'Hugh, you better get out. I've got you beat.' They were a delightful couple and fun to be with.

"Both Stuckey and Ethel loved the Derby and horse racing. They would pull that car into Louisville, back it up to the main street, and it couldn't have been any nicer. We had some of the best food you ever saw, and certainly it was the best company in the world. Jean and I went with Stuckey and Ethel to a baseball game out in St. Louis one time, too," Senator Gillis declared. "And we went to the Orange Bowl once."

Senator Gillis recalled, however, that business was never really far off Stuckey's mind. "Even when we were at the Derby, he called Eastman every day to keep up with his business."

Senator Gillis and Stuckey became friends when they served in the Georgia General Assembly together. Stuckey was elected to the House of Representatives in 1959 and served until 1964, representing Dodge County. Senator Gillis first served in the Georgia Senate in 1957-1958, and since 1963 has served continuously. Earlier he was elected to the House of Representatives where he served in 1941-1944, and again served there from 1949 to 1956. Ethel and Jean Gillis were congenial and became good friends also.

Friends of the Stuckeys can scarcely reminisce about Stuckey the man without mentioning Ethel, his wife. She played a key role both in Stuckey's business relationships and in his social activities. After all, his good friends also were frequently his business associates, and they were Ethel's good friends as well. Ethel was always at her husband's side when they entertained friends, and she planned the fabulous parties at their St. Simons Island home that so many remember with nostalgia.

Ethel Mullis Stuckey was an attractive, tall, slender, dark-haired woman. Her main hobby was playing bridge, a diversion she enjoyed throughout her life, even in her later years. She liked nothing better than a good game of bridge with friends, unless it was a good game of poker. Despite her complete support of her gregarious husband, Ethel is remembered by some as a rather private person, with a natural sense of reserve.

Moody also recalled going with Stuckey to the Georgia-Florida football game in Jacksonville. "Stuckey would get a whole bunch together—Tom and Billie Greene, Jack and 'Woo' Huckabee, Dot and me—and Stuckey would have Boots to drive the men in his Cadillac, and Ethel took the ladies in her Cadillac. We would meet at the Mayflower Hotel where he had rented a suite of rooms, had a piano moved in, and the suite would be stocked with all kinds of sandwiches, snack foods and liquor. If you went with Stuckey, you did not worry about a thing. It was all beautifully organized down to the last detail. Same way with the Kentucky Derby. He loved the Derby."

In a similar nostalgic vein, Moody in a personal interview recalled a trip he made with Stuckey to the World Series. "He got our tickets through the Cincinnati Ball Club. Stuckey, Tom Greene, (then president of the First National Bank in Macon) Jerry Achenbach (then president of Piggly-Wiggly), and I, four good friends, went to New York, stayed three or four days and had more fun as Stuckey's guests."

According to Senator Gillis, Stuckey was a good sportsman, and he loved hunting and fishing, and also liked to play cards and to have fun. Of these, Billy believes that it was cards that his father really preferred.

It is said that Ethel was known occasionally to become piqued at Stuckey and his friends on one of these trips. She would sometimes show her spunk by rounding up all the ladies in the party and taking them back to the private train car in Louisville. They would have a good game of bridge and leave the men to their own devices.

Senator Gillis recalls a trip to the Orange Bowl with Stuckey. "I will never forget that trip," he reminisced. "We were supposed to leave the Eastman airport at 11 a.m. We were to fly in a twin engine Aztec plane which belonged to Stuckey, and he had a good pilot. We got over there and the weather was bad. We could tell it was too rough to fly, so we called Macon, and they said just to wait.

"We waited an hour, called again, and they said that if we could see a little hole in the sky looking south, we could get through that hole and it would be clear. The hole, however, closed up before we could get through it and we were in the worst storm I ever saw. I have never seen such bad weather. The plane would fall several hundred feet straight down, and then we would go up and back down again. I don't see how that plane stayed together. We got down about Alma,

Georgia, and the pilot radioed and they said we could not stay up there any longer. We were flying at 8,000 feet and they told us to drop to 5,000. We did but it was still real rough. We finally got out of the soup down about the Florida line. Of course, we enjoyed the game, and we flew over to Freeport, and had some fun over there. We came back into the Miami Airport. Billy, then a Congressman, was with us, and we had Jack Flynt, too, and maybe another Congressman. We had to wait out in the field and got into a line for about thirty minutes. I went up to ask if it would help any if we had a U.S. Congressman with us—they said it sure would, and I told them we had three with us. They got us through real fast. Coming back, we checked the weather and there was a storm between Miami and Georgia. After what we had been through, we decided to stay another night. Our wives were not with us, and they never did really believe our story about the bad storm. They thought we were just having a good time and wanted to stay another night."

Without exception, Stuckey is described as "ambitious, smart, courteous, and with a good personality." Those who knew him best say repeatedly that they "never knew anyone who did not like Stuckey." Although Stuckey thoroughly enjoyed a good joke, he did not tell jokes very often. He was not above pulling pranks on his friends at times, however.

An example is remembered by Elva Lee Connell, Stuckey's secretary. "Governor Carl Sanders was Mr. Stuckey's good friend," she recalls. "One day he knew that Governor Sanders would be coming by the office, and he took a framed picture of the governor off his office wall, took the photograph out, and replaced it with a sign that said, 'Carl Sanders Was Here,' and put it back on the wall. He enjoyed the look on the Governor's face when he saw the sign. Of course, the moment the Governor left, the picture went back up. Mr. Stuckey was proud of his friendship with Governor Sanders."

Sometimes a joke backfired, but Stuckey was a good sport when this happened and enjoyed this, too. The Rev. J. B. (Jake) Hutchinson, pastor of the Eastman United Methodist Church in the 1950s, became Stuckey's good friend, and remembers a particular occasion when Stuckey's reputation for pulling pranks backfired.

"I was driving from Eastman down to Epworth by the Sea at St. Simons Island," Rev. Hutchinson recalls. "I had gotten to Baxley when Stuckey overtook me, hailed me down, and I stopped. Boots was driving his car and he had his brother-in-law, Lewis Mullis, then the sheriff of Dodge County, with him. They were going to St. Simons, too, where Stuckey had a home. Stuckey said, 'Jake, let Boots drive your car, and you come ride with me.' I got in the car with them.

"Very shortly, a man in a big car started following us, honking his horn, and got us to pull over. It was a very prominent man in Baxley who was Stuckey's friend. He started out with a few choice epithets, saying, 'Where in the ---- are you ----'s going?' Stuckey tried to intervene by saying, 'This is a Methodist preacher with us, Jake Hutchinson.' The man, figuring that Stuckey was pulling his leg, said, 'Like --- he is. No self respecting Methodist preacher would go anywhere with you two ---'s.' Things got worse before Stuckey convinced him that I was indeed a Methodist preacher."

Rev. Hutchinson said that Lewis Mullis never let Stuckey forget this incident. The Baxley man was terribly embarrassed when he found out the truth, and many years later he was still apologizing to Rev. Hutchinson.

Rev. Hutchinson said that Stuckey was faithful about attending church when he was in town. "Of course, he had to travel a lot and would be away and not at church. I would tease him about it. I remember being a bit apprehensive when I was going to the Eastman church when I found out that a millionaire was a member. But he and I hit it off from the beginning and became good friends. I never had a better friend in my life than Stuckey."

Stuckey never had an outright failure with any of his many endeavors, as far as is known. As to the secret of his phenomenal success, various friends and acquaintances offer ideas and comments. "Hard work was the number one ingredient for Stuckey," Senator Gillis said. "And Ethel was right there with him. Then, too, he was diversified. He believed in good management, and he hired a lot of good people. Most of his people were his good friends and good business people. His style of management was different—today it is strictly business and folks don't know your family and don't care. It's hello and good-bye today. Stuckey knew his people wherever they were, and he looked after them personally as long as he could. That was what was so good for his franchise owners. He saw to it that the stores were managed properly."

Emmett Barnes, Macon real estate developer and close business associate and friend, remembers similar trips, including some to St. Simons, Miami and the Kentucky Derby. He also believed that Stuckey enjoyed all these activities.

Barnes said, "If you were a good friend of Stuckey, he would get you a store. He got me two, both in Colorado. I was very fortunate to get them—I put out $5,000 in each store, and he got me the financing at $100,000 each. The stores were supervised out of Eastman, and they would get a manager for each store who reported to Eastman (headquarters).

"Stuckey worked hard and played hard. He was a successful man. If I had to pick the ten most outstanding friends I have had in my lifetime, Stuckey would be high up on the list. He was a good man, a trustworthy man. When he said something, you could count on it."

In reflecting on his relationship with his good friend, Barnes commented, "I would say that Ethel contributed a lot to Stuckey's success. I would say that Ethel had a pretty good influence on his business. Stuckey did not believe in working all the time—he was by no means a workaholic. He and Ethel liked to have their parties down at St. Simons, and they were great parties. They would play poker—I am not a poker player—but he and Tom Greene would play poker."

Barnes recalls that "every year prior to Stuckey's and Tom Greene's deaths, we would go down to Miami. He and Tom would stay at Miami Villa and I would stay with my family over at Miami Beach. I had my son Emmett with me, and he must have been about 16 years old. We were going to the races the next day and he gave Emmett $20.00 to bet with. Stuckey was one of the richest people in Georgia, but he never lorded over any of us and never let on that he had more money than anybody else. He had a good time. He had good friends. His motivation was—I think—that he just liked to make money."

Stuckey had friends who spanned a wide age range, many of whom were considerably younger than he was. He was regarded as "ageless," and because of his vitality, energy and zest for life, age was not important in his relationships. One close friend, many years his junior, said, "It never occurred to me to think about his age."

Also bearing out the fact that Stuckey liked to be with people is a comment by W. T. (Duck) Moody. "Stuckey never wanted to be alone," he remembers. "He always wanted people around and very seldom did you see him by himself."

Stuckey loved children, and children loved him. This included his own children and later his grandchildren, and his employees' and friends' children. There was an affinity between him and children, and he liked having them around. His important board meetings were always open to children who happened along. For example, his grandson, Russell Dean Franklin, III, would sometimes sit in on very important meetings, being very quiet and still.

Always present on the various trips and parties that Stuckey planned for his friends was his constant companion, Boots Fluellen. Moody recalled, "When we would be traveling around, we broke the color barrier long before integration came. We would stop at a hotel or motel, take a suite, and say that Boots needed to take our baggage up there. Then Boots would just stay with us, although it was not permitted in those days. Boots would either have a room or sleep in the room with us. We would bring food to Boots because he could not go in the restaurants with us."

A longtime Stuckey, Inc. employee, Jack Lott, who in later years was secretary-treasurer of the corporation, remembers, "Boots was a little hard to understand if you did not know his personality. Stuckey always looked after Boots. One time Stuckey gave him an old Chrysler that was in pretty good shape. We had credit cards (for the business) and did not pay much attention because Boots always bought gasoline for Stuckey. I finally noticed that Boots was also using the credit card for himself, for car washes, gasoline, etc. and when I asked Stuckey, he did not know anything about it. When Stuckey talked to Boots, he said, 'When you gave me the car, I thought you were going to pay for my gas, too.'"

Boots had learned to "draw" his name, but he could not really write. He managed to sign well enough for credit card usage and endorsing checks, however. He learned to write "B-o-o-t" but never did manage to get the "s" on his name. It is entirely possible, as many have surmised, that Stuckey may have spoiled Boots a bit, but Boots repaid him manyfold in his devotion to "the boss man."

Boots made trips all over the country for Stuckey, despite not being able to read traffic signs or a map. He delivered parcels to Billy in Washington, D. C., and went to New York City on errands. As one family friend said, "He couldn't read or write, but he sure could drive a car."

Elva Lee Connell remembers an occasion when Boots was allowed to borrow Stuckey's Cadillac for a specific occasion. The automobile was beautifully kept—Stuckey required Boots to keep it carefully washed and waxed and the interior was meticulously clean at all times. "Someone riding with Boots burned a hole in the front seat," Elva Lee recalls. "Boots, in telling about the incident, said, 'That night I prayed that morning wouldn't ever come.' He knew he had to return the Cadillac and confess to Stuckey that a hole was burned in the front seat." Elva Lee said that Stuckey examined the damage, noted Boots' extreme distress, and immediately solved the problem. He simply bought a new Cadillac, and Boots was off the hook.

In recalling Stuckey's love for Boots, Emmett Barnes commented, "Boots was always there to wait on Stuckey. If ever an employee loved his boss, Boots loved Stuckey. Boots stayed in the house or the office and drove Stuckey's car. He was a valet and a true friend."

Lynda said that one of the most important people in her father's life was Boots, and he was constantly with him. (Almost every person interviewed had similar comments about Boots.) "Boots was very special," she remembered, "and he always ate at my parents' home. He was Daddy's right arm."

Stuckey shows off a unique Christmas gift from his staff. Wearing his new overalls, with a red bandanna, he is ready to demonstrate that he can still plow a straight furrow if only he had a mule.

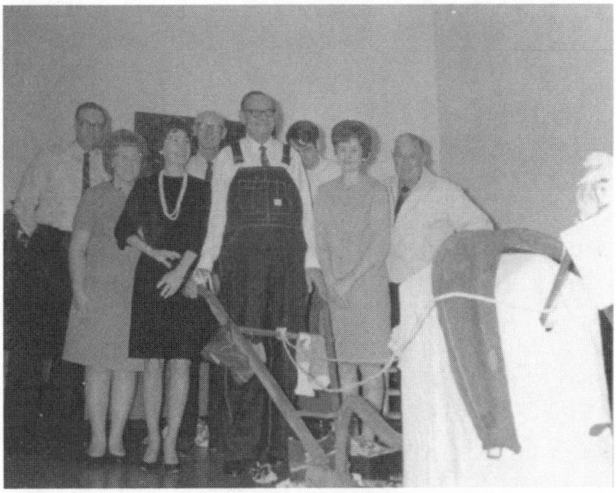

Admiring Stuckey's Christmas gift are staff members who are thoroughly enjoying the joke.

Stuckey, center, poses with his brother, Felix, left, and his half-brother, Frank, right.

The Stuckey home in downtown Eastman
is owned by the Stuckey family today.

Stuckey moved his young family from the country to this home in Eastman circa 1940. The house is no longer standing.

This is the old Williamson home where Stuckey and Ethel lived with his grandmother, Cora Lee Williamson, for some years after their marriage. The home, used for arts and crafts now, is owned by the Stuckey family.

Then Georgia Governor Jimmy Carter shakes Stuckey's hand after administering the oath for service in the Georgia House of Representatives.

Stuckey at his desk in Eastman.

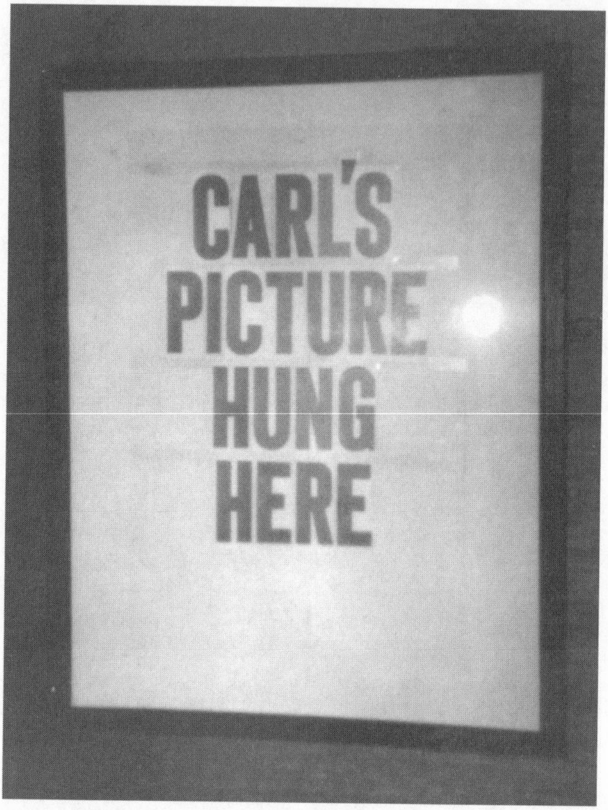

When Georgia Governor Carl Sanders was coming to visit, Stuckey hung this sign, as a joke, in the spot on his office wall where the Governor's picture usually hung.

Stuckey, center, poses with his staff circa early 1960's.

Candy kitchen employees stand behind Stuckey and some of his staff, circa early 1960's.

The legendary Boots Fluellen, third from left, figured prominently in Stuckey's life. Here, Boots is joined by three friends.

Baseball legend Joe DiMaggio, second from right, was the center of attention when he visited Stuckey's in Eastman. With him, left to right, are Edwin Methvin, Dewey Mullis, Stuckey, and Russell Franklin.

This is the first home of Stuckey's in Eastman.

This is an example of an "early-years" design used in Stuckey stores.

This is a later design used for Stuckey stores.

This is typical of the store design used during the latter period of Stuckey's life.

Stuckey, Ranger J. F. Beauchamp and Jack Warren look over some of Stuckey's timberland.

Stuckey's pecans and candy were first sold at this roadside stand, the first Stuckey "store." It is still owned by the Stuckey family. Stuckey and a friend pose by the stand.

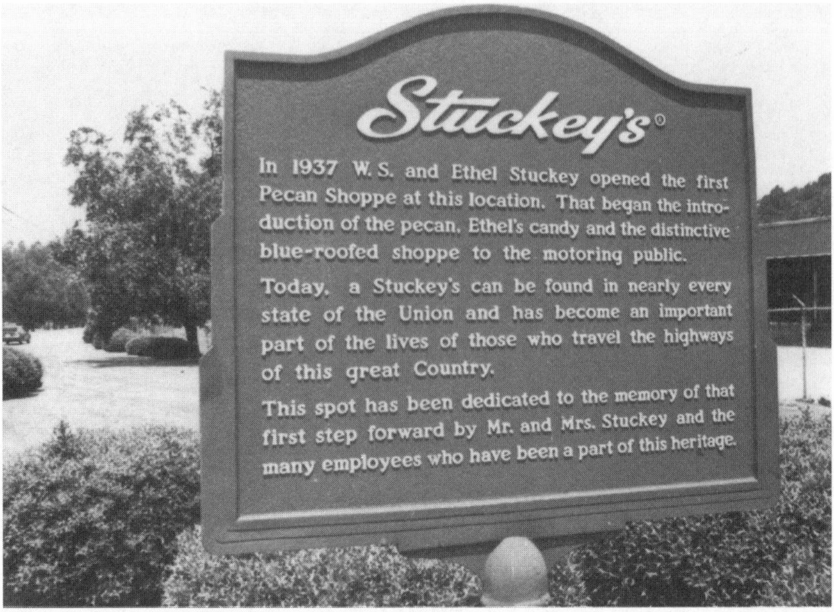

This sign marks the location of the first pecan shoppe in Eastman, Georgia.

Relaxing on the patio at Stuckey's St. Simons Island home are: left to right, Fred Wynn, Carlisle Minter, Stuckey, and Millard Greene.

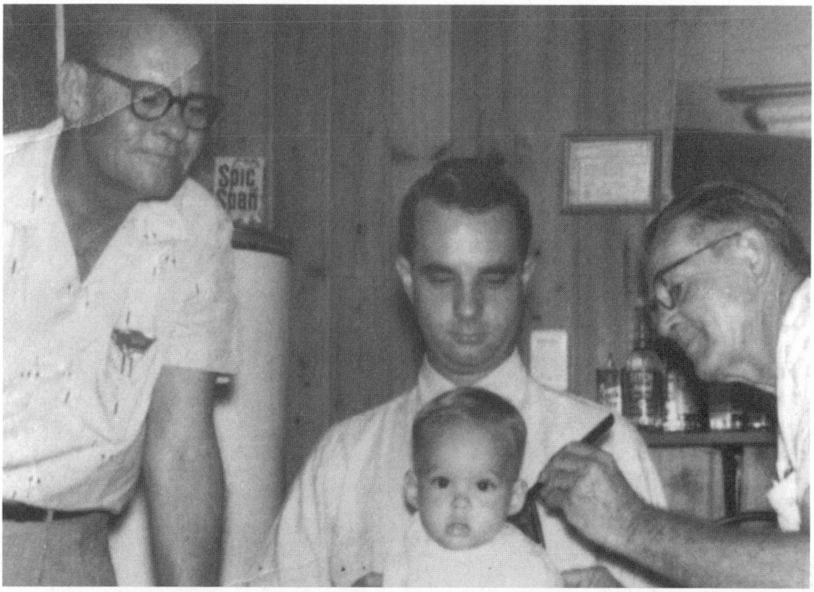

It is a momentous occasion when Williamson Sylvester Stuckey III, "Little Billy," gets his first haircut while a proud grandfather, left, and father, center, look on. The barber is Mr. Pruett in Eastman.

The Stuckey family focuses attention on two grandsons: Russell Dean Franklin III, and Scott Maloy Stuckey, right. Looking on, left to right, are Stuckey, Ethelynn Stuckey, standing; Billy, seated: and standing, Lynda Stuckey Franklin, and Ethel Stuckey, and Dean Franklin, seated.

In Commemoration
of
W. S. STUCKEY SR.
WHO GAVE UNSELFISHLY OF HIMSELF, HIS COMPANY AND TIME TO FAMILY, ASSOCIATES AND FELLOW CITIZENS, WHO INFLUENCED COUNTLESS LIVES THROUGH BUSINESS AND HIS GENEROSITY, INCLUDING THOSE LIVES OF THE NATION'S HIGHWAY TRAVELERS.
STUCKEY'S FRANCHISE ADVISORY BOARD
EASTMAN, GEORGIA
FRED A. MILLER JR.
J. TOL THOMAS III
EUGENE M. FLOWERS
W. S. BROFFITT
WILTON D. HARRINGTON
JANE B. WINGATE
W. T. MOODY
WALTER DYAL
E. J. PARKER
S. ERNEST VANDIVER

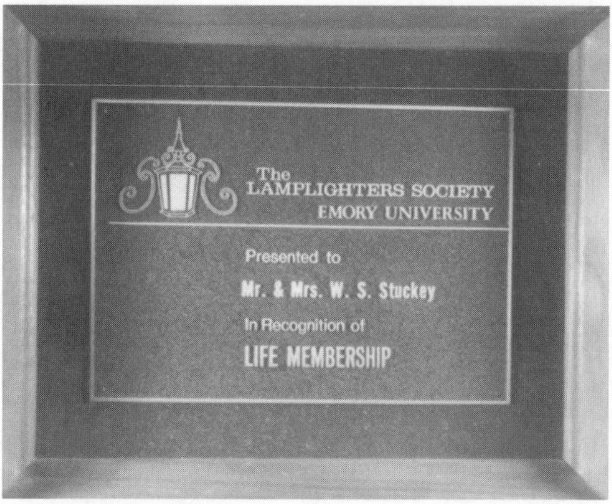
The
LAMPLIGHTERS SOCIETY
EMORY UNIVERSITY
Presented to
Mr. & Mrs. W. S. Stuckey
In Recognition of
LIFE MEMBERSHIP

Stuckey's
GREAT AMERICAN AWARD
Presented To
W. S. Stuckey Sr.
APRIL 20, 1976
Atlanta, Georgia

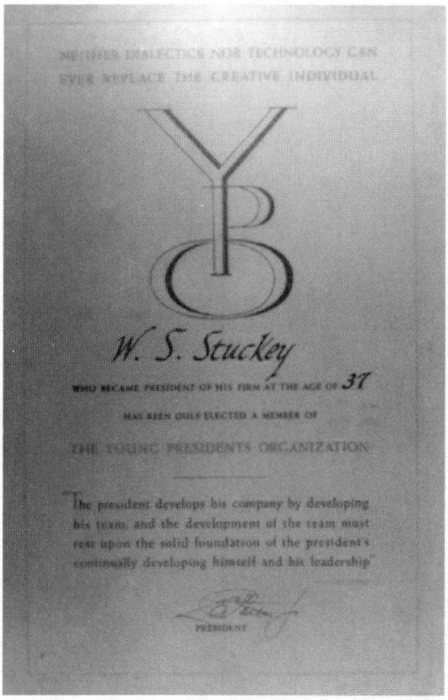

NEITHER DIALECTICS NOR TECHNOLOGY CAN EVER REPLACE THE CREATIVE INDIVIDUAL

YPO

W. S. Stuckey

WHO BECAME PRESIDENT OF HIS FIRM AT THE AGE OF 37

HAS BEEN DULY ELECTED A MEMBER OF

THE YOUNG PRESIDENTS ORGANIZATION

"The president develops his company by developing his team, and the development of the team must rest upon the solid foundation of the president's continually developing himself and his leadership"

PRESIDENT

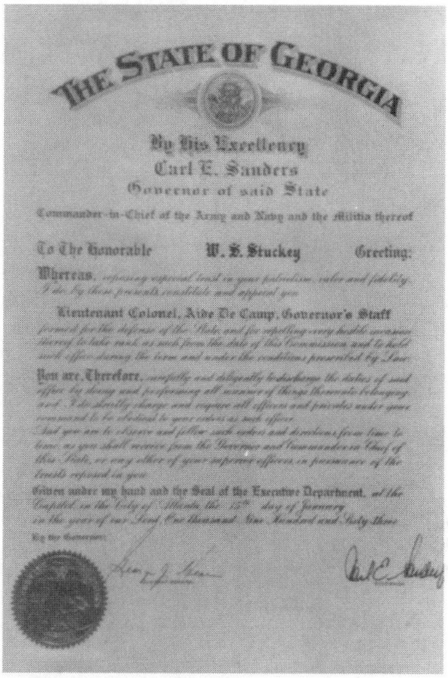

THE STATE OF GEORGIA

By His Excellency
Carl E. Sanders
Governor of said State
Commander-in-Chief of the Army and Navy and the Militia thereof

To The Honorable W. S. Stuckey Greeting:

Whereas, reposing especial trust in your patriotism, valor and fidelity, I do by these presents constitute and appoint you

Lieutenant Colonel, Aide De Camp, Governor's Staff

formed for the defense of the State, and for repelling every hostile invasion thereof to take rank as such from the date of this Commission and to hold such office during the term and under the conditions prescribed by Law.

You are, Therefore, carefully and diligently to discharge the duties of said office by doing and performing all manner of things thereunto belonging and I do strictly charge and require all officers and privates under your command to be obedient to your orders as such officer.

And you are to observe and follow such orders and directions from time to time as you shall receive from the Governor and Commander-in-Chief of this State, or any other of your superior officers in pursuance of the trusts reposed in you.

Given under my hand and the Seal of the Executive Department, at the Capitol in the City of Atlanta the 15th day of January in the year of our Lord, One thousand Nine Hundred and Sixty three

By the Governor:

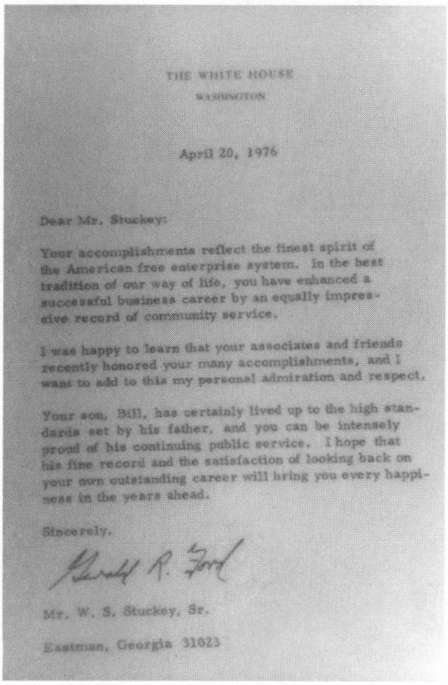

THE WHITE HOUSE
WASHINGTON

April 20, 1976

Dear Mr. Stuckey:

Your accomplishments reflect the finest spirit of the American free enterprise system. In the best tradition of our way of life, you have enhanced a successful business career by an equally impressive record of community service.

I was happy to learn that your associates and friends recently honored your many accomplishments, and I want to add to this my personal admiration and respect.

Your son, Bill, has certainly lived up to the high standards set by his father, and you can be intensely proud of his continuing public service. I hope that his fine record and the satisfaction of looking back on your own outstanding career will bring you every happiness in the years ahead.

Sincerely,

Gerald R. Ford

Mr. W. S. Stuckey, Sr.
Eastman, Georgia 31023

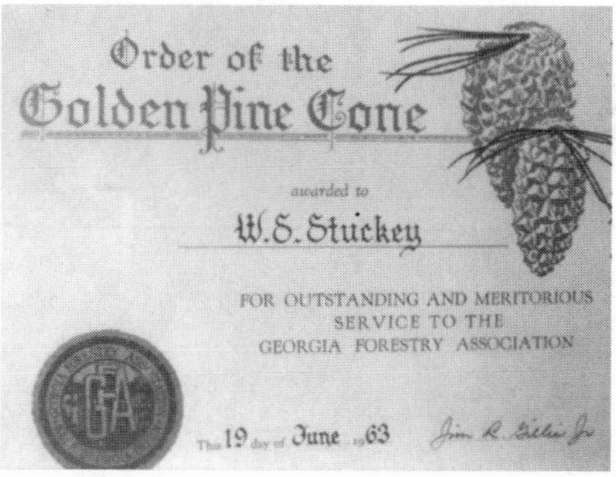

Order of the Golden Pine Cone

awarded to

W. S. Stuckey

FOR OUTSTANDING AND MERITORIOUS SERVICE TO THE GEORGIA FORESTRY ASSOCIATION

This 19 day of June 1963

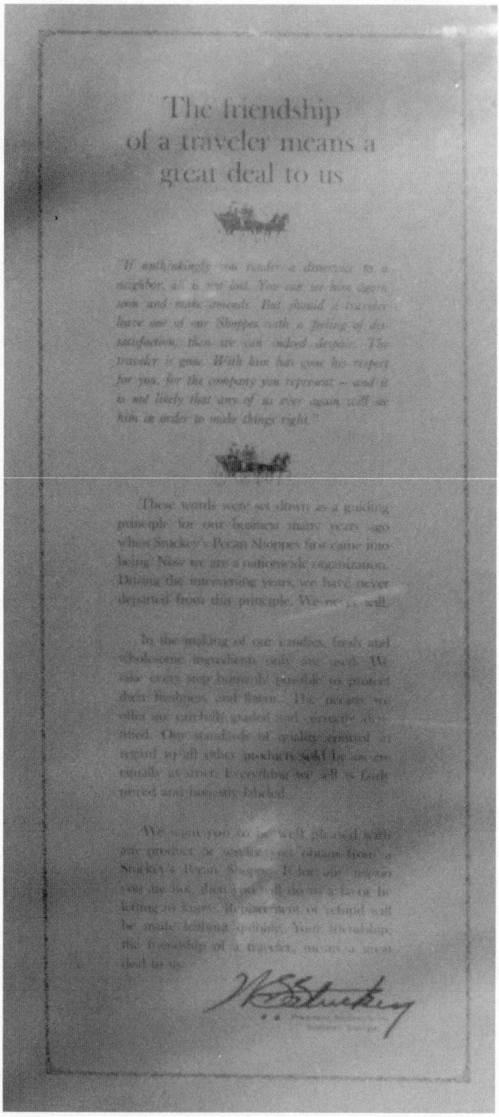

The Stuckey motto was hung in all the Stuckey stores.

This billboard, typical of those Stuckey used, welcomed motorists to Stuckey's in Eastman. In the early years bill boards were the main advertising used.

Billboards such as this drove travelers crazy, but still enticed them to stop at the next Stuckey's.

A last reminder that Stuckey's is just ahead.

Williamson Sylvester Stuckey, Jr. (Billy), age ten, and Lynda Stuckey, five, one of Stuckey's favorite photographs of his children.

Stuckey family members pose on the front steps of the new Stuckey Timberland building in 1996: They include: Billy Stuckey, Ethelyn Stuckey, Russell Franklin, Amy Elizabeth Franklin, Stuart Stuckey, Billy Stuckey III, Catherine Stuckey, Stephanie Stuckey Weber, Gerald Richard Weber, Scott Stuckey, Beverly Stuckey Franklin, and Jay-Gould Stuckey. Lynda Stuckey Franklin, not pictured, was the photographer.

The new Stuckey Timberland headquarters is located
on Hawkinsville Highway in Eastman.

In front of the new Stuckey Timberland building is this sign.

Chapter 8

DODGE COUNTY OR A PIECE OF THE MOON

Lynda and Billy remember spending endless time with their father, riding around the countryside, as he looked at his farmland and timberland. Later, he would take his grandchildren on these jaunts. He seldom went anywhere, even to a convenience store to pick up some tomatoes that Ethel needed for supper, without taking a child or a grandchild along. Or he would spot a friend on the street, stop, and take him along wherever he was going.

Billy declared, "My father's great loves were: his grandchildren, Dodge County, and his grandmother, probably in that order." However, there is strong evidence that his children and his wife also ranked high on his list of affections.

"He had a great love of the land, and if he could have lived in New York or anywhere in the world, he still would have chosen Dodge County," his son said. "If someone had wanted to give him a piece of the moon, he would not have wanted it if it was not in Dodge County."

During the years that the Stuckey stores were growing so rapidly, Stuckey continued to buy Dodge County land almost compulsively. He also bought some property in adjacent counties, but it was Dodge County that drew his love. Good farmland and poor farmland—he bought it all, and turned some of it into pecan orchards and the rest was planted with pine trees. At this time pine trees, in particular, were not considered to be very profitable. Even those who knew Stuckey well looked upon his devotion to buying up land as something of a hobby in which he indulged.

Although Stuckey was considered by many to be the eternal optimist, he had his occasional "down" times. Duck Moody remembered several times getting an early morning telephone calls when Stuckey would say, "Duck, this is Stuckey, I've got the blacks. You busy today? (By the "blacks," he meant that he was feeling down, grumpy, and low.) Come on down and talk to me." Moody continued, "I would ride on down, get there before dinner (lunchtime) and go out to the house with them for a big meal—fresh vegetables, the best food in the world. When I would get there, he would begin to tell me what he had the blacks about. Usually he would end up laughing about it and would feel better."

Moody also remembers, "Stuckey was always 'neat as a pin.' He wore the finest clothes he could buy. He liked for his people to do the same. He did not like sloppy people, and he always did business with good folks. He would say, 'Do not do business with sorry folks.' That was his motto, in a way. He had no patience with 'sorry' folks."

Stuckey had a lot of influential contacts, Moody remembers, and they were "from the President on down." Then, on the other hand, Stuckey had countless ordinary individuals who went to him in confidence with their various problems, and he always had time to help them and give them advice.

Moody recalled that Stuckey frequently talked about his early years and the hard times he endured. He would tell Moody that "sometimes all I had to wear on a date with Ethel was a clean pair of overalls and a jumper."

Many observers attest to the fact that Stuckey and Franklin made an excellent team. Stuckey liked the public relations and promotion aspects of the business. He liked contact with people, but he was not a detail person. He left the management and administrative details to Franklin whose inherent abilities along these lines served the business well. A writer once described Franklin as Stuckey's "alter-ego." Franklin was said to be able to perceive problems and solve them before they happened. "Stuckey and Franklin were a perfect balance for each other," a longtime friend said.

"Stuckey was primarily a trader," Franklin remembers. "He really liked to trade and swap, and he could always trade well. It was one of his greatest attributes. He could handle money and trading better than he could handle people. He simply could not stand to fire someone. He did not like to manage. He was a very smart man, and he knew how to make good deals. He was a master at getting credit—he had to be because people had to trust him. This was his forté—he could get money to expand the business. He was affable and friendly, and people liked him. He was highly motivated, ambitious, and he liked power. He could make money at the drop of a hat. Yet he was a very tolerant and kind man."

Stuckey, as his son described him, was a man of contrasts and contradictions, however. Franklin believes that Stuckey was actually rather shy, although this was not immediately obvious. And certainly his close friends did not observe any timidity in his personality.

"Stuckey was not aggressive in the sense that he would go into a meeting and control it," Franklin recalls. "He was very quiet in a meeting situation. He never said much unless he really had something to say. He was not a public speaker, but he could be very dogmatic once his mind was made up. Most of the time he had me to conduct his meetings," Franklin said. "When he was in politics, he really did not have to make public speeches. He might say a few words, but he always had people with him who could speak. He really did not like public appearances."

Franklin confirmed what various others have said of Stuckey. "He was an imposing physical presence, and this gave him a definite psychological advantage."

Jack Lott, who worked for Stuckey from 1954 in various capacities, eventually becoming secretary-treasurer of Stuckey Timberlands, commented, "Stuckey always exerted authority. He was THE BOSS."

Stuckey did not like to sit behind a desk. He was an "outside man." He worked by appointment, however, and was conscientious about performing necessary office tasks. His staff did not know what an eight-hour day was and coffee breaks were unheard of. But after his people had worked extremely long and hard, he rewarded them with a few days of enjoyment and relaxation at St. Simons Island.

Lott continued, "Stuckey liked to make money. He enjoyed the game of it, and he liked the risk and give and take of the stock market. Many people after the Depression were afraid to take risks, but Stuckey was different. He was a risk-taker, and when he made a mistake, he learned from it without dwelling on it, and simply did not make the same mistake again."

Another trait which was constantly and consistently attributed to Stuckey by numbers of people who knew him well was the fact that Stuckey had only one way to treat people—fairly and courteously. Whether he was dealing with a worker on the line in the candy plant or a banker or a top politician, he did not have to shift gears, because his approach was the same. He liked people, and it showed. He put complete faith and trust in his people, and, knowing this, they dared not do less than their best.

Fred Miller, Jr., vice president for finance and personnel for Stuckey's, commented, "If Stuckey had something to say, he said it, and he did not beat around the bush. I heard him one time call Carl Sanders when he was governor of Georgia regarding a pending bill to outlaw billboards in Georgia. He did not hesitate or spare any words as he let Governor Sanders know how displeased he was. Stuckey liked Governor Sanders—he only talked that way to folks that he liked." Apparently he could do this and get away with it, because his friends never seemed offended by his frankness.

Miller described Stuckey as a "self-made man" in the sense that does not happen any more. "He had some money to go to Georgia (the University of Georgia) but did not graduate. He went from law school to plowing a mule—that's one extreme to another. He was a hard worker. He was not a detail man, but he was an idea man, a public relations man. He had other people to handle the details. He would say to me, or to some other member of his staff, 'You know I don't like to fool with these damn things—you take it and handle it.' And that would be that. He would dismiss it from his mind, and trusted you to do the job, once he gave it to you. He let you alone and let you do the job then. He put a lot of trust and faith in his people."

Miller said Stuckey used a unique method to hire his people. "He would hire by the seat of his pants," Miller said, describing the way Stuckey would make personnel decisions. "He kept his salaries minimal, but gave people an opportunity to buy into a store. This did two things—it made them a part of the business, and it kept his payroll low so that he could expand."

It was part of his philosophy to find and keep good people. On the other hand, it has been speculated that he really hired ordinary people, but made them extraordinary by his unique style of management and the quality of leadership he provided.

Miller mentioned that among the people who had franchises or interests, were Duck Moody, Dr. Calder Clay, Tom Greene, Dr. John O'Shaughnessey, Dr. Herb Olnick, Georgia Senator Hugh Gillis, Herman Talmadge (at one time Governor of Georgia and later a United States Senator), and Emmett Barnes. And numbers of Stuckey employees had interests in stores, along with members of the Stuckey and Mullis families. As mentioned earlier, his old friend, John King, later his yard man, at one time also had an interest in a Stuckey's store. Elva Lee Connell remembers that King had very little education and could not understand why his store was not profitable right at first, so he sold it.

However, he had the same opportunity as anyone else. Connell herself owned several stores. And the legendary Boots Fluellen also had an interest in a store at one time.

Stuckey had a paternalistic concern for his employees. Connell said that Stuckey bought up some land near a park in Eastman and divided it into lots. Many of his employees bought lots, financed mostly by Stuckey, and a number of them still live there today. Jim Thomas, the candy plant manager; Jack Lott, then the bookkeeper; Jack Southerland, a warehouse employee, Hubert Hardy and Elva Lee Connell were among those who owned homes there, thanks to Stuckey. "We (my husband and I) would probably never have been able to buy a home without his help," Elva Lee said. She and her husband live in their comfortable, attractive home today.

Illustrative of the affection which his employees felt for Stuckey is a carefully planned special Christmas gift they gave him one year. Stuckey had a collection of stories about his mule, from the Depression years, and of his days plowing it in the fields. He enjoyed telling the stories over and over again—he loved a good story.

The employees spent a great deal of time and effort getting a pair of denim overalls, a red bandanna, and a plow for his Christmas present. When these were presented to him, Stuckey was so delighted that he went off and put on the overalls, tied the bandanna around his neck and posed for a picture taken by Jack Lott. He got many a chuckle and much pleasure showing the photograph to his friends.

Lott remembers another Christmas, around the late 1950s. "It had been customary for the employees to take up a collection to buy Stuckey a Christmas present, and he decided to stop the practice. He came up with the idea of setting up a foundation, and each year employees would take up a collection and put it in the foundation. He would match it, and later on, funds also came from other sources. Primarily, the foundation's purpose was to make loans for higher education at low interest rates. It was not restricted to the children of employees. The requirements were stringent—if you could afford education any other way, you did not get it. And soon after leaving school, students had to begin repayment. But the Tax Reform Act made it all so complicated that it was discontinued. The Board of Trustees voted to liquidate the fund, and all money went to Emory University for a scholarship fund in theology which had already been established by Stuckey."

Regarding this endowed scholarship, Rev. J. B. (Jake) Hutchinson remembers how the idea for it originated. He had noted Stuckey's generosity to many causes, and suggested to him that he consider establishing an ongoing scholarship fund to educate ministers. Rev. Hutchinson arranged a meeting with the dean of the Candler School of Theology, the development officer at Emory, and Stuckey. Rev. Hutchinson had warned the dean not to mention a specific amount of money, but to let Stuckey name the figure. After the project had been outlined, Stuckey asked, "How much do you want?" The dean stammered around a bit, and Stuckey replied, "Tell you what, I'll give you $10,000 now and by the end of the year I will make it $100,000." Rev. Hutchinson recalls that this was a tremendous amount for those days, far exceeding what the dean would have expected and accepted.

Rev. Hutchinson also recalls that Stuckey always gave generously to the church. "The members would set a goal for the church budget, and I would be worried about meeting it. They would tell me not to worry, that they'd raise what they could and Stuckey would make up the difference. And he did. Apparently this was customary. I was concerned about it because I thought that every member should do what he or she could, but they knew that they could count on Stuckey. He did this also with the building fund for an education and recreation center. He simply took up the slack and gave whatever was needed to complete a campaign."

Rev. Hutchinson said, "Stuckey always respected my being a minister and treated me with the utmost respect. I never heard anyone make a derogatory remark about Stuckey. Ethel was a fine woman, too, and a good worker in the church. She attended Sunday School and was a member of the missionary society. She visited those who were sick or in trouble. She was a good woman." On one occasion when Stuckey was serving in the Georgia General Assembly, he made arrangements for Rev. Hutchinson to serve as chaplain of that body.

Throughout his life, Stuckey was a firm believer in, and supporter of, higher education. He strongly encouraged it among his employees, and demanded that his own children get college degrees. In general, he was considered a "soft touch" for charities and various causes, and realized that he was probably exploited sometimes, but he did not worry about it.

Lynda said, as others have expressed it, so many of her father's good works will never be known because he did many good deeds anonymously, not wanting credit or recognition. "In my opinion, he simply did not worry about being exploited—he knew he was a soft touch and he knew that everybody else knew it, too."

Rev. Hutchinson remembers that one Christmas Stuckey called him and asked him to stop by his office. When he got there, Stuckey asked, "Jake, what are you getting for Christmas?" I told him I hadn't given it much thought. Stuckey said, "Well, I want you to go to Joseph N. Neel's in Macon and pick out the best suit of clothes they've got and charge it to me." Rev. Hutchinson was stunned. He said he finally stammered, "But I don't know the folks at Neel's. Could I go to a store in Savannah instead?" Stuckey agreed. Rev. Hutchinson said, "I went to Savannah and bought a good looking suit of clothes, courtesy of Stuckey."

Stuckey had the reputation of going first class himself, and he liked for all his friends to go first class, too, many have said.

Most of Stuckey's good deeds were done quietly, without fanfare. Many times they were completely unknown even to his family. But sometimes word of his private philanthropy surfaced and became known, and Stuckey would be rather embarrassed.

"There was this black guy from Dodge County who had above average intelligence," Billy recalls. "My father paid his way through a medical school in New York back in the 1940s when such a thing was unheard of in the South. My father was not in the formal sense a deeply religious man," Billy said, "but in his own way, he did a great deal of good, much of which was known only to the recipients of his generosity. He used to say that it was not on the vote of his peers that he expected to get in the pearly gates."

Elva Lee Connell remembers well that, whether a request was from a Holiness Temple or a black church or a school fund raiser, Stuckey would either reach in his pocket for a bill or tell her to write a check. He never said "no" to any cause.

Reflecting on her father's phenomenal success and his lifting himself up by his bootstraps, Lynda observed: "It is probably not possible, or at least very, very difficult today to do what my father did. My parents enjoyed it all, even the hard times."

Although it was not customary in those days for females to be involved in business, Stuckey involved Lynda in as many aspects of his business as possible.

"When I was real young, they would get a wooden Coca-Cola crate and turn it upside down and I would stand on it. I would take the nougat center of the log rolls and throw it in the caramel. A lady would be on each side of the pot holding cooking forks and after I threw them in, they turned the nougat center over, then pulled up the caramel and put the candy in a box. I also helped with making divinity and pralines—a little bit of all of it. "My father saw that when I went in the plant like this that I worked and did not mess up or simply be in the way. He always paid me a little—I liked to earn money."

Elva Lee Connell, when cleaning out her boss's desk following his death, found a note from his daughter that he had carefully saved. It said, "Daddy, I owe you fifty cents." She does not recall whether she ever paid for this I.O.U., but probably not, since he had saved it. Most likely, though, he saved it out of sentimentality.

When Lynda was twelve to fourteen years old, she worked with her aunt, Mary Lizzie Mullis Winburn, in the accounting department, helping with the daily reports. "My mother's family all worked for my Dad in some way," Lynda said. "Another of my mother's sisters, Aunt Ruth, and her husband, Uncle George, were store managers, and I would go with them and work in their store. Several of my mother's nieces and their husbands also worked with Stuckey's."

She recalls that her father always said that "women don't necessarily make good business people because their emotions get in the way of their good business judgment." Lynda continued, "Even though this sounds (today) rather chauvinistic, it was simply the thinking of the period. Nevertheless, I have always been on guard against this. His words are always in the back of my mind."

She remembers sometimes being rather jealous of the demands on her father's time, and telling him that he put others ahead of his family. "He really did not," she remembers. "He was very gentle, a big old teddy bear, and I could wrap him around my little finger."

Stuckey's love for his grandchildren was always evident, too. He enjoyed them and took a great deal of pride in them and their accomplishments.

Mrs. Verna Ragan of Eastman, a nonagenarian, the widow of the late Claude Alexander Ragan, recalls Stuckey with a particular sense of nostalgia. Her husband was the banker who backed Stuckey in his fledgling days, and Stuckey was forever grateful to him. Ragan met an untimely death, and Stuckey acknowledged his indebtedness to him by paying special attention to Mrs. Ragan for the remainder of his life.

Mrs. Ragan reminisced, "His quality of pride was strong. I kept books for General Mercantile Co. in Eastman for 16 years, and after my husband died, I still worked with my husband's partner. Stuckey needed someone to work for him, and I heard that he wanted me, but he wouldn't ask me because he did not have a good office—when they came in with a load of pecans, they would dump them in the middle of the floor. I did not mind, and I worked for him a number of years, also worked some in the new warehouse, at least eight or ten years in all, but only in the buying season, the fall. I kept books for him and signed every check for him. Stuckey had so many good qualities. He had high standards, and had a respect for the poorest person. He was as good a boss man as you could want. But he did have a temper. He would sometimes hide out in my office from persons he did not want to see."

Because his beloved mentor, Ragan, died at such an early age, before Stuckey achieved much success, Stuckey was never able to repay his indebtedness to him directly. Elva Lee Connell believes that this influenced Stuckey throughout his life, and that he tried to help others in the way Mr. Ragan had helped him. He never refused to co-sign a loan for one of his employees or to lend assistance to the poorest person who came to him.

In his own way, Stuckey was a philanthropist. A member of the Committee of One Hundred at Emory University, he contributed generously to the Methodist school. As noted earlier, he was a generous supporter of the Eastman Methodist Church. But it was his anonymous acts of charity which he preferred and about which details will never be fully known. He always supported local causes, such as the Dodge County High School Gymnasium fund, to which he gave $10,000. Also, in 1960 he made available to Dodge County 4-H Club members 10,000 pecan trees to be planted during a five-year program plan. Five pecan trees were given to each 4-H-er who agreed to buy five more trees, and plant and care for them. This was well publicized in the local newspaper.

Active in civic and community endeavors, he became in his later years an honorary member of the Eastman Rotary Club. He had served as president of the Jaycees, and he was a member of the Civil War Centennial Committee in 1959. He was a member of the prestigious Young President's Organization. Among the varied positions of leadership which he held was the presidency of the tourist division of the Georgia State Chamber of Commerce, and he was a member of the Governor's Mansion Committee. He was named to the Georgia Advertising Commission created by Governor Herman Talmadge in 1954.

One of the highest honors, in his estimation, was appointment in November 1962 to the Board of Directors of the First National Bank in Macon, serving until his death. An important result of this service was the close lifetime friendships he formed with a number of board members and bank officials.

Elva Lee said that at Christmas every year Stuckey sent boxes of candy to all employees at the courthouse, at the hospital, and at Southern Bell in Eastman. And Mrs. Ragan was always on his candy list for Christmas, even the last Christmas before Stuckey's death early in the New Year.

Mrs. Ragan recalls that when Stuckey moved the building for Stuckey Timberland downtown (after he had sold the business to Pet, Inc.), he bought some Kennedy rockers and placed them inside the reception area. This was a spot from which he could see all over town. When he saw Mrs. Ragan walking along the street, he called her to come "rock and talk awhile." He did this with many people he knew, always keeping his finger on Eastman's pulse, knowing what was going on. He was interested in people and politics, but most of all he was interested in what happened in Eastman and in Dodge County.

Emmett Barnes said despite the fact that in his heyday Stuckey was one of the richest men in Georgia, he never changed at all, but remained exactly the same.

Stuckey's other favorite spot was the swing on the side porch of his home, right in the middle of Eastman. He loved to sit there in his later years. From here, he could also see much of Eastman. And sooner or later almost everyone in town passed by. "Every time I go by, I still think of him sitting there swinging," Elva Lee said.

Emmett Barnes summed up his feelings about his friend quietly and reflectively, "In my opinion, Stuckey was a great man."

Chapter 9

STUCKEY'S BECOMES A HOUSEHOLD WORD

By the late 1940s and early 1950s, tourism was steadily increasing and Stuckey was primed to take advantage of it. He began to open even more stores—or stations as he called them—at carefully selected sites in the southeast. By 1952, Stuckey Pecan Shoppes were located in Florida, Virginia, Tennessee, North Carolina, South Carolina, Mississippi, and Georgia.

In the early years, Stuckey had no high-powered marketing and public relations consultants to advise him on site selections and the creation of an image by his business. But in his own way, he was a marketing and public relations expert, from whom the so-called "experts" might well have taken lessons.

His innate sense of marketing was a curious mixture of common sense, an entrepreneurial spirit, and his inborn love of risk-taking. He always did his homework, made his own careful traffic surveys, and had strong opinions about how to attract and keep the tourist trade. He stood staunchly by his belief that tourists would spend more on their way home from Florida than en route, and he enticed them—increasingly—with his ever-present series of billboards which informed a captive audience of motorists that the next Stuckey's was twenty ...

then nineteen ... then eighteen ... and so on, miles away. He never abandoned his carefully worked out plan for strategic locations of the stores. He sent his workers to state capitals to ferret out road histories and to determine where future highways and interstates would be built, to enable him to make informed decisions about where to build stores.

There is a family legend about how Stuckey selected the locations for his stores. After drinking several cups of coffee, he had Boots drive him until he needed to make a rest stop. And that was where he would build a store.

While admittedly an interesting story, it nevertheless has a grain of truth, because Stuckey deliberately contrived to provide for his customers' total comforts and needs, all in one easy stop at a Stuckey's store.

In later years, Stuckey had marketing and advertising directors, and made use of the services of prestigious Atlanta public relations and marketing firms. But in the beginning he simply followed his instincts which led him on an unerring path. His son, Billy Stuckey, has said that his father's motto was, "Early to bed, early to rise, work like hell and advertise." He loved a challenge, as many who knew him attest.

In reality, Stuckey was a pioneer in many of his business practices. Remarkably, he was light years ahead of others in his generation in the implementation of innovative offerings to the public, ideas which would be commonplace in less than a quarter of a century.

Although it was not then called fast food, he was the first to offer quick-food service in his stores, which were one-stops for multiple needs long before convenience stores were dreamed of.

In the South, Stuckey's was the first location of its type to allow blacks to use rest rooms. Stuckey was also a pioneer in the mail order catalogue business when this was unheard of for a business such as Stuckey's. Truly, he was a generation ahead of his time with many of his creative endeavors, although these practices would be emulated by his competitors in years to come.

Stuckey was full of ideas and gimmicks to entice another customer into one of his stores. His fertile mind was always at work. At Stuckey's, weary travelers could find multiple services—food, gasoline, candy, souvenirs, gifts, and rest rooms. His idea of providing fast-food service was totally new, and customers loved getting food orders quickly so they could be on their way. He saw clearly the immense possibilities that the interstate provided, and he was the first to locate his stores there. When he began his mail-order business, with catalogues, many predicted failure because it had not been done before. Instead, it was highly successful as were all his endeavors.

Many of Stuckey's ideas have been incorporated into daily life today—a convenience store seems to be located on every corner; fast-food outlets are found in every city and small town, and they have sprung up like mushrooms at exits along all interstates; catalogues selling everything from cheeses to Christmas ornaments clog everyone's mailbox. Truly, Stuckey was far ahead of his time, breaking new ground with new and unique marketing techniques. There is no doubt that Stuckey possessed a rare creativity which served him exceedingly well.

For example, recognizing the importance of keeping the children of his customers happy, he had coloring books available for them in all his stores. He saw to it that the mail order catalogues were attractive and enticing, drawing in a whole new group of customers. Stuckey's patrons received cards entitling them to two cents a gallon discounts on gasoline. He touted boxes of candy as Christmas gifts from employers to employees. Delta Airlines served Stuckey candy to its passengers. He worked out a deal for travel club members to receive discounts at Stuckey stores. He did not miss a trick in promoting sales, and even started his own newsletter, *Sweetalk,* promoting his products all over the country long before newsletters became the trend.

He began a "Sweet Set-Up" Fund Raising Division to sell candy to civic organizations interested in raising funds. A limited number of products were personalized with the name and logo of the organization imprinted on the overlap. By 1960, this division, which began as a direct mail business, had about seventy representatives in thirty states. As a result of this success, two shifts were put on in the Eastman plant. The mail order business was sending out between 150,000 and 200,000 gift catalogues annually.

Stuckey employed basic psychology in his unique approach to marketing. Believing that people like to trade where a lot of other people trade, he had his employees to park their automobiles in front of his stores so that it would appear that business was heavy.

With the exception of some souvenirs and the sandwiches served in the snack bars, every product sold at a Stuckey's store was either produced by, or packaged by, the Eastman plant. The number of Eastman citizens employed by Stuckey's steadily increased throughout the post-war years, and by 1960, 250 townsfolk were employed there. Indeed Stuckey's employees were described as "growing like Mrs. Rabbit's family."

On the national scene, Senator Joseph McCarthy was getting some attention in the news as he advised President Truman that the State Department was "riddled with Communists." In 1950 there were one million television sets in the United States, and one year later the number had increased to fifteen million. This made it possible, instead of just reading about important events, such as the McCarthy accusations, actually to "see" them as they occurred.

In 1951 North Korean Forces broke through the 38th parallel, taking Seoul, and rejecting American truce offers. Communist-ruled North Korea invaded South Korea and in June captured Seoul. Douglas McArthur was appointed Commander of the United Nations forces in Korea, and UN forces recaptured Seoul. The United Nations asked member countries to aid South Korea, and the United States and other countries sent troops. The war ended on July 27, 1953 when the Korean Armistice was signed at Panmunjon, and the United States and Korea signed a mutual defense treaty. But the effects of this war did not reach deeply into the daily lives and routines of most Americans as had World War II.

Republican Dwight D. Eisenhower was elected as the 34th President in 1953, and re-elected in 1956. The Democrats were out of power for the first time since Roosevelt was inaugurated in 1933. Meanwhile, the Stuckey plant in the 1950s was processing approximately 54 varieties of candies and nuts. A great deal of the equipment was either hand-built or greatly modified to perform tasks unique to the Stuckey operation.

Because of Stuckey's rapid expansion, the need to service an ever-increasing number of stores presented a monumental transportation problem. This prompted Stuckey to enter the private carrier realm in 1950 by investing in his first air-conditioned tractor and refrigerated trailer. It was extremely important that precious candy cargoes arrive on schedule and in good condition. As time went on, he expanded this phase of the operation and maintained a sizable fleet of trucks.

Most of the units operating under Stuckey franchises were owned either by the individual store managers or by other investors. By 1960, for example, the Stuckey family owned only ten of the 115 stores outright, with a half interest in ten other stores. Meanwhile, some 1,000 persons were employed by Stuckey's and $5 million worth of candy was being manufactured annually. Although this fact was not officially confirmed, Stuckey's was believed to sell more pecans at retail than any company in the world.

The stores were all selling Stuckey products and Texaco gasoline, both good sources of revenue for Stuckey. The franchise deal called for Stuckey's to make the candy and distribute all items at a profit, handle advertising and promotion, keep the books, provide supplies and replace signs as needed. During this period Stuckey acquired a Piper twin-engine Aztec plane for his personal use. He enjoyed the luxury very much.

The Stuckey name was becoming increasingly well known and highly respected. In the July 6, 1953, issue of *Newsweek*,

Stuckey's received the following mention: "By now millions of tourists who roll toward Florida for winter sun and summer breezes know the scenery very well—pines, palms, motels, and Stuckey billboards." In this article, Stuckey's is described as "interesting, unusual, and a very friendly place. The noble pecan holds sway here."

Stuckey expanded his horizons and began to place advertising in nationally known and prestigious publications such as *Newsweek, Reader's Digest, The New Yorker, Look, Saturday Evening Post,* and *Better Homes and Gardens.* But his old standby, billboards, remained the foundation of his advertising. It was reported that "the only way to avoid a Stuckey's and still get to Florida would be to detour through Alabama." And, although the stores lined every artery leading from Georgia to Florida, there were plenty of stores in Alabama, too, and in most southeastern states. So, detouring through Alabama might not have been a sure-fire way to avoid a Stuckey's while still getting to Florida.

Much free exposure came to Stuckey's through trade publications, such as *Trux,* a magazine for southern truckers, and the *Goodyear Triangle* because Stuckey used Goodyear truck tires. They touted him as "the Georgia farm boy who parlayed a $35 investment into a $16 million a year candy business." At that time the company was shipping 50 tons of candy bi-weekly to 115 stores, and tourists were offered 54 varieties of candy, plus pecans, jellies, hams and souvenirs. This was in 1962. In 1963 Sunset Magazine described Stuckey's as "the roadside stand that grew into a multi-million dollar business."

In *Southern* Post in 1964, an article was headlined: "Stuckey's Saga—From Pecans to Pagodas." This referred to Stuckey's venture into Carriage Inns. Pagodas were used on roof tops of the inns. Another publication said, "From a few handfuls of nuts on a crate top by the highway to a multi-million dollar company." Writers for various newspapers and publications and advertising copywriters had a field day with the Horatio Alger story. *The Candy & Confectioners' Journal* wrote full-fledged features about Stuckey and his business, and he got attention in the publications of the National Association of Travel. *The Peanut Journal and Nut World* in May 1953 pointed out that Stuckey's was doing $1 million per year in business. Stuckey was at that time Chairman of the Tourist Promotion Division of the Georgia State Chamber of Commerce. Suddenly Stuckey's was getting constant mention in varied publications, a priceless commodity. For him, success was building even further success.

Stuckey was quoted frequently in the early years as saying he had more money invested in billboards than in inventory. In the 1960s, $200 was invested in each sign—and it took $100,000 a year to maintain the billboards. His sign crews were constantly on the road.

As mentioned earlier, Stuckey placed a parrot in the Eastman store on a whim. It was an instant success and a remarkable drawing card. The unusually loquacious parrot entertained droves of children who remembered him season after season. Eventually, almost every Stuckey's store featured either a parrot or a mynah bird. The parrots remained important fixtures in Stuckey stores until health department regulations eventually intervened and decreed they be removed.

On March 4, 1953, a special Stuckey's edition of the *Times Journal* in Eastman heralded the opening of Stuckey's new $125,000 candy plant and office building on the McRae Highway. The special edition contained the largest number of photographs ever published in one issue of the newspaper which contained 58 pages, making it also the largest edition ever published, and containing seven full-page advertisements plus many smaller ones.

The building was described as being "of steel and masonry construction and containing 10,000 square feet of floor space." It was also described as being "one of the most modern of its kind in the United States." Murals of lush pecan groves covered the walls of the reception room.

The opening of the new candy plant attracted widespread attention, and many congratulatory telegrams and letters were carefully saved in the Stuckey Scrapbook which Ethel Stuckey conscientiously kept. Among the treasured letters are greetings from Bob Hope and Bing Crosby who expressed their appreciation for gifts of Stuckey candy. In the *Macon Telegraph and News,* Macon, Georgia, an editorial lauded the opening, and various other newspapers and publications gave it coverage. The congratulatory telegrams came from people, both famous and those unknown.

The new building was not large enough to serve Stuckey's rapidly growing needs for long. The business's phenomenal growth prompted the building of a $100,000 addition to the plant two years or so later, in 1955.

Commenting on his father's uncanny sense of marketing, Billy remembers, "Every time I rode with Dad, he would count out-of-state tags. He was simply obsessed with keeping a tally on tourists. A lot of it was simply common sense—he learned by trial and error. As has been said, he would build his stores on the right hand side of the highway—or east side—going north, on a curve, in a deliberate and calculated manner of attracting tourist trade. He would also have the employees to park in front of the stores and even would bring in old cars so the places would look busy. It's a funny thing—today employees have to park out of the way in parking garages."

Billy, a graduate of Georgia Military Academy, received the Bachelor of Business Administration degree from the University of Georgia in 1956, and then was graduated from the University of Georgia Law School with the LL.B. degree in 1959. He was a member of Sigma Alpha Epsilon Fraternity, Phi Delta Phi fraternity, and the Gridiron society. Billy was married to Anne Armistead of Atlanta, Georgia on December 24, 1956.

On the national scene, Senator Joseph McCarthy continued his "witch hunt" for Communists. At first, he was not taken seriously, but by 1954 he was causing quite a stir as television audiences watched. On another front, Dr. Jonas E. Salk had developed an anti-polio serum, and countless families breathed easier as the ever-present threat of crippling polio—or "infantile paralysis"—was eliminated. Immunization became even easier when an oral vaccine against polio was developed by Albert Sabin in 1956. And in 1957 Dr. Seuss thrilled a generation of children with his "Cat in the Hat." Future generations of youngsters would be equally enchanted with this book and others he would write.

A day when Lynda was about fifteen years old stands out in her memory. This would have been in 1955. Her father called and asked her to come down to the office. Important matters were always discussed in his office, but she was totally unprepared for the subject this time. It was to change her life completely.

"When I got there, he said, 'Lynda, come fall you are going to boarding school.' I was shocked. 'Sir?' He repeated it. 'I have made the arrangements,' he said. 'You are going to Stratford Hall in Danville, Virginia.' I replied, 'But, Daddy, I don't want to go.' He said, 'It does not matter whether you want to go or not.'" Lynda did not question her father's authority. He simply told her what to do and she did it. He looked at her and said, "It's settled then."

He saw his daughter's unhappiness, however, and said, "I tell you what—I will give you a new car to drive if you will go on and accept this."

"He used to bribe me a bit. So he got me a new 1955 Chevrolet Belair, black with white interior, a beautiful little coupe. I thought it was the hottest car around. The rest of that summer I would take it to the beach and my friends and I would ride around with the windows rolled up so everybody would think it was air conditioned even though we were burning up. I was so proud of that car," Lynda remembers.

When fall came, she was off to Stratford Hall, and not very happy about it. "Mother drove me up there, and I cried all the way," Lynda said. "When I got there, I did not like it at first. It was strange to live in a dormitory, three to a room, with one bath for everybody on the hall. After about a month I really started to enjoy it, and I learned so much—how to get along with people and being in a controlled environment was good for me. I spent three years of high school and one year of college there. I am glad that Daddy made me do it, and later on I told him and my mother this." Later Lynda attended the University of Georgia where she was a member of Kappa Kappa Gamma Sorority.

Remembering her days at Stratford Hall, Lynda recalls that when her father was in that part of the country, he came by Danville, Virginia, and spent a night or two. "He would take some friends and me to dinner, and it would be such a special time," she remembers. "He came fairly often, and my mother came all the time. I was at home on holidays and I was in touch with my family all the time."

Tension was growing as the desegregation of schools was attempted in the south. In 1955 blacks in Montgomery, Alabama, boycotted segregated bus lines. Civil rights activists led marches of protest. A minister named Martin Luther King led with a nonviolent approach. In 1956 the USSR launched its first earth satellites, followed in 1957 by the United States satellite, Explorer I. By the early 1960s both Russia and the United States had put men in space, and the Space Age had begun.

Lynda Stuckey and Dean Franklin grew up knowing each other very casually through the association of their parents in Stuckey's. Lynda was away at boarding school through her teen years, and Dean was at boarding school in Castle Heights, Lebanon, Tennessee. Both worked in the Stuckey's warehouse one summer, but they did not get to know each other. Certainly dating never crossed their minds. When Lynda was a freshman in college, her brother Billy and his then wife, Anne, were giving a Christmas party which all of the family and Stuckey business associates would attend. Dean, then at a wedding in Atlanta, called home and his mother, Millie Franklin, told him about the party. He probably should have a date, Millie said. Thinking a moment, Dean asked, "Is Lynda going to be home?" Finding that Lynda would be in Eastman, he told his mother, "Well, call her for me and ask if she will go with me to the party." Millie did. Lynda accepted. But after that, Millie did not make any more dates with Lynda for her son. He made them himself.

Lynda and Dean continued to date over the next few years. Eventually, both the Stuckey and the Franklin families recognized that the relationship was becoming increasingly serious.

Meanwhile, Stuckey's love of Eastman never faltered. He was active in civic and community endeavors, locally at first, but later expanding his service to include statewide and even larger positions of leadership. At one time, he served as president of the Eastman Jaycees, and as president and director of the Clearing Bank in Eastman and of the Eastman Cotton Mills. Life was indeed good for Stuckey and for everyone associated with him.

Chapter 10

THE HALCYON DAYS OF THE EARLY 60S

In 1960, John F. Kennedy was a candidate for the presidency of the United States. Stuckey, always a staunch Democrat, headed Kennedy's campaign in South Georgia, and there was much rejoicing when Kennedy was elected as the 35th and youngest president. Stuckey and Ethel attended the inauguration ceremonies in Washington.

Thus began a period in the early 1960s which might well be described as the "halcyon days." It was as though a fresh wind blew across the country. A young president with a new vision brought the promise of a bright future. A spirit of excitement and change permeated the land.

Even popular music took a definite new turn when a group from England called the Beatles created a new disease called "Beatlemania" which swept the country. Young teenagers drove their parents to distraction with their stereos blaring incessantly, "I want to hold your ha-a-a-n-d," "Hard Day's Night," and "Yesterday."

In the early 1960s Stuckey brought Joe DiMaggio, the legendary Hall of Fame baseball player, to Eastman as a special guest of Stuckey's, Inc. His visit was in connection with completing arrangements for the Monette Company to serve as worldwide distributors for Stuckey products. DiMaggio was head of the public relations department for the company. While in Eastman, he visited the Dodge County High School baseball diamond and autographed baseballs for many persons. It went without saying that a great deal of positive media coverage was given to DiMaggio's visit, as evidenced by the Stuckey scrapbook.

When John F. Kennedy was assassinated in November, 1963, Stuckey shared the country's profound shock and sorrow. Vice President Lyndon B. Johnson became the 36th president, and subsequently was elected to a full term in 1964.

In contrast to the earlier days, Stuckey began to use Atlanta advertising agencies to direct his marketing and promotional activities. His half brother, Frank Stuckey, handled these responsibilities which included the whole gamut except billboards, with a budget of $300,000 annually. This was considered a huge amount in those days.

By the late 1950s and early 1960s Stuckey's business interests grew, and as he delegated more authority, he was able to take on more activities. He and Ethel went on a People-to-People goodwill tour of Georgia Agriculture Leaders to Europe and the Soviet Union. They sailed on the Queen Mary, and visited many countries—France, Monaco, the Italian Riviera, Italy, Switzerland, Germany, Holland, Belgium, Denmark, Sweden, Norway, Scotland, England and other countries. They attended the International Exhibition of Sugar Industries in Amsterdam. Stuckey and Ethel were now enjoying the fruits of their labors, and life was good.

Stuckey always gave candy samples to whoever requested them—to Halloween carnivals, for example, and not just in Dodge County but in other Middle Georgia counties as well. The candy plant was a popular place for tour groups which were conducted regularly in large numbers. School groups especially enjoyed touring the plant because each student was given a generous sample of candy. Many children wrote Stuckey thank-you notes after their visits. Typical was a little boy who wrote: "Dear Mr. Stuckey: I enjoyed the tour of your candy plant. Thank you for the candy. It was good but I sure was sick the next day."

In the midst of the phenomenal success of the stores, Stuckey continued his lifelong practice of pursuing additional business interests. As has been mentioned, his business interests were wide and varied. These business endeavors included at various times automobile dealerships, a Ford tractor dealership, a funeral home, a furniture store, a railroad crosstie business and at one time he owned a juke joint which catered to blacks. (They didn't have anywhere to gather and have a drink and enjoy themselves in those days, he once said, by way of explanation.) Other interests at various times included a used car business, a scrap iron business, restaurants and motels, oil wells in Texas, pecan trees, timberland, farm crops of corn, peanuts and oats, and cattle and hogs.

His innate love of the land was overriding, however, and throughout his entire life, he continued to acquire farmland and later timberland. He remained diversified, but his love of the land superseded his belief in diversification. Some have described it as a hobby or an avocation, albeit an expensive one. Whatever his motive, by 1960 he owned 10,000 acres of farmland where he employed good conservation practices, restoring part of it for growing cotton, corn, soybeans and grain, and putting part of it into good pastureland for raising herds of beef cattle. On the less productive land he planted pine trees, almost as an after-thought. Much later, the family holdings of timberland would expand to 30,000 or more acres, and this would eventually become an extremely valuable investment. A total of approximately 100 sharecroppers lived on the Stuckey land at that time in the early 1960s.

Billy Stuckey said, "Dad started Stuckey Timberland, having no idea it would do so well. Timber has always been a commodity in this part of the country. But his first love was always the farm. I have ridden over more tracts of land with him. Every time he had a bit of spare time, he wanted to ride over his land. He especially liked to go out in Bleckley County to some farmland he owned there."

Russell D. Franklin, executive vice president of Stuckey's for many years, recalls that in the beginning no one in Eastman anticipated what Stuckey's would eventually grow to be. Thoughtfully, he continued, "I must confess that I did not think about the size of the business either. It was just step by step, store by store. I never visualized it as becoming a big chain." In retrospect, Franklin does not believe Stuckey realized the potential in the beginning either.

Mrs. Verna Ragan, who remembers well the early days when Stuckey's was beginning, said, "Stuckey's was a godsend to Eastman. We didn't have much else except the cotton mill."

During the 1950s, Stuckey started several new corporations. On July 1, 1956 Stuckey Timberland, Inc., a corporation, was formed which includes all land and timber holdings of the family; along with Stuckey Investments Corporation, formed to include all family-owned commercial property, mostly in Eastman. In 1958 another corporation, Stuckey Pecan Company, was formed to augment the other corporations. It was established for the purpose of purchasing pecans in season and storing them. Two large freezers were built, and this enabled the business to buy pecans in good years, carrying them over to assure a plentiful supply in bad seasons.

Other new companies included Signs & Plastics of Georgia, Inc., a division of Stuckey's that occupied a 40,000 square foot manufacturing plant and employed 35 persons initially. The company manufactured molded plastic merchandising signs and displays and had four departments, designing, molding, fabricating and erecting. He had two full-time crews building signs and sometimes four crews would be painting signs across the territory. He even had his own printing presses, and once when the presses of the Eastman newspaper broke down, this company printed the weekly newspaper.

The fact that Stuckey's timber interests were growing during those years caught the attention of Susan Myrick, editor of the farm page at the *Macon Telegraph and News*. On Sunday, September 22, 1957, she had an article headlined: "W. S. Stuckey, Eastman, Grows Pine Trees on Nearly 10,000 Acres." He also had one of the largest and best-tended pecan orchards in the state, in addition to his farming operations which included some 750 acres in row crops and grains, raising 300 head of beef cattle, and 600 to 700 hogs each year.

The Stuckey venture into the motel business was on the horizon, but did not develop until the early 1960s. The first Stuckey's Carriage Inn opened in Eastman in 1960. The pilot 40-unit motel was located near the firm's headquarters. It featured a heated swimming pool, 150-seat dining room, a meeting room for 75 persons. The plan was to offer motel franchises first to current store owners and then to others. Billy Stuckey was president and chief executive officer of the new motel chain, and Russell D. Franklin was executive vice president. This motel served as the prototype for six others.

In retrospect, Billy recalls, "It is admittedly difficult to be objective about one's father. At times it was not easy to be his son. But there were advantages. I certainly did not grow up in a log cabin. We had a nice home in Eastman, a home in the mountains, and another at St. Simons Island, and we had a boat. I remember many good times spent with my father. He loved his family."

Billy also remembers some frustration in working for his father. "I was young and had some new ideas. For example, I figured it would be efficient to put in an IBM system, and before it had a chance to prove itself, people who ran it convinced him that it would not work, and he got rid of it. He absolutely would listen to anybody—nobody was better than anybody else, in his opinion. I would come up with some great (I thought) idea to increase productivity, and any hourly worker could walk in his office and say it wouldn't work, and he would throw the idea out," Billy recalls.

Although Billy has sometimes been described as a "carbon copy" of his father, this is not true. But there are strong similarities and common family traits. It is not unusual for a strong father and a strong son, sharing many of the same characteristics, to have differences of opinion, as Billy pointed out that he had with his father. The very similarities of their temperaments almost insured that this would be the case.

In looking back upon his father's life, Billy comments, "He was really very liberal for his day. He was very much a capitalist, but also a populist, one of those contradictions that apply often to him. If you look at where people were in that day and if you take the racial animosities into consideration, Southerners were basically populist. My father believed in Social Security, health care, and in the redistribution of wealth. He would explain in great detail why nobody should vote for a Republican."

Like most fathers and sons, the Stuckeys had their moments, good ones and those not so good. "But I can truthfully say that I enjoyed working with him, and I learned a lot. If something did not go right, he let you know immediately. He was fair, though, and there was a balance," Billy said.

"Dad always went to bed early, but he got up at 4:30 a.m. and was out of the house by 5 or 5:30 a.m. He was part of a group of men, County officials and business leaders who met at the County Prison every morning, drank coffee and caught up on all the news. The farm heritage was strong with him. Almost everybody he knew got up early like that," his son commented.

Billy said that his father was a conceptual person not concerned with details. Instead, he would call upon whatever experts he needed for the task at hand. "He would get an idea and then find the right people to carry it out," Billy declared. "He surrounded himself with good people. He really had remarkable people working for him. He would say that you should find the best person to do a job and then get out of the way and let him do it. This was a philosophy he used all his life, and it worked."

Billy declared that one of the most ingenious ideas his father came up with was a gauge for figuring the cost of gasoline, as mentioned earlier. "Country folks would sell gas for say, 19.9 cents per gallon, and they could not figure out what the total was. So my father got a great idea, he thought. He had a brass gauge made up which could be attached to the gasoline pump, and it would give the total of the sale. But he did not keep a sample gauge for himself. He tried all his life to find one, but he never could, although he tried hard."

In many ways, Stuckey was a man of contrasts and contradictions, a complex personality. But one thing remained consistent—he enjoyed the entrepreneurial spirit, and he liked to make money. He truly liked to see other people prosper too, as has been said, and he took great delight in seeing his family and friends have their investments do well.

In the meantime, the candy business flourished. It was estimated that by 1960 his franchisees were making a minimum of $50,000 a year profit and maximum of $150,000. This was considered exceedingly good for the period.

The Stuckey scrapbook contains a wide assortment of clippings indicating that media recognition for Stuckey's continued to come from many unexpected sources. An example is an article by syndicated columnist, Leo Aikman (updated in the Stuckey scrapbook), recapping an article by Gene Methvin of the *Washington Daily News,* written for his hometown newspaper, the *Vienna News,* in Dooly County, Georgia. (Methvin was later on the staff of *Reader's Digest.*)

Methvin wrote about a visit to the historic Civil War battle site at Gettysburg where he went to the stone wall on Cemetery Ridge and looked down "on the mile-high, rising bare field over which Pickett charged." He wandered around, reading plaques and asked himself: "What brought these fine southern men, these brave Georgians, to this faraway hillside?" Methvin said that his cheeks were hot, his eyes wet, and he was mad. Then he drove off the hill to the site where the Confederates had re-formed and fallen back. "And, there, bless us all," wrote the native Georgian, "a couple of hundred yards farther ... stood a Stuckey's Store, with its succulent fudge, divinity and pecan rolls, all bearing the blatant, 'Made in Eastman, Georgia' label for all the damn Yankees to see."

The able writer ended the column this way: "So, after 96 years, the Georgians still hold a bit of ground on that hard-fought battlefield. There is some justice after all. Stuckey's Last Stand. Last Stand North, that is, for the time being." Methvin's reference to the battle's taking place 96 years previously (1863) indicates that the date of the column was 1959.

Another phase of Stuckey's life came through his entering politics. This decision surprised some of Stuckey's friends and closest associates. He had a phenomenally successful candy business, plus a number of other businesses which were doing well. Why did he decide to run for the State Legislature? The question was debated and discussed by many people. The real reason may be one that not even the candidate himself knew fully, but it had to do with his love of Dodge County and that region of the state, and of his wanting to make a contribution in this arena. It may also have had to do with his love of power and authority, and once in the race, his old determination to win permeated the campaign. One of his colleagues has said, "Stuckey hated to lose (at ANYTHING) worse than anybody I ever saw."

He was elected to the Georgia House of Representatives, representing Dodge County, and served there from 1958 to 1964, always as a Democrat. During his service he was a member of the highway, industrial relations, ways and means, industry and state of the republic committees.

Stuckey enjoyed his years in the General Assembly, according to all reports, and his record was outstanding. He was influential, and served the citizens of Dodge County well. Added dividends were the lasting friendships that he acquired while serving in the Legislature. An undated clipping in the Stuckey family scrapbook carries the headline: "All Seven Bills

Introduced in the recent Sessions of General Assembly by Stuckey Have Been Approved and Signed by the Governor."

Regarding his father's political experience, Billy commented, "My father served as John F. Kennedy's campaign manager for South Georgia. But Kennedy was not very popular down here then. My father was strong for Kennedy, though. I remember going out and picking up Orville Freeman, later Kennedy's Secretary of Agriculture, and Dad took him over South Georgia campaigning for Kennedy. He went to Kennedy's inauguration in 1960."

Stuckey's service in the Georgia Legislature took him away from Eastman and away from the day-to-day involvement with his business, and even when the Legislature was not in session, he received many telephone calls and spent a great deal of time meeting with and talking to constituents. As with all his ventures, Stuckey approached his work in the Legislature with enthusiasm and whole-hearted dedication and commitment. He was never lukewarm about anything in his life, and he gave at least 110 percent , and maybe even more, to his service as a State Representative.

In 1961, the marriage of Billy Stuckey and Anne Armistead Stuckey ended in divorce. They had two children: Williamson Sylvester Stuckey, III, and Stuart Anne Stuckey. On June 2, 1963 Stuckey's daughter Lynda was married in Eastman to Russell Dean Franklin, Jr., the son of Stuckey's longtime business associate and friend. Billy Stuckey and Ethelynn McMillan Stuckey were married on June 16, 1963.

In the first few years of the 1960s, Stuckey's candy business continued to expand—a far cry from the little roadside shack in 1937. At the end of his sixth year in the General Assembly, Stuckey did not offer for re-election, but he always looked back upon this service with nostalgia, and he maintained a strong interest in politics throughout his life.

Chapter 11

BIG DADDY DAYS

If ever a man doted upon and adored his grandchildren, it was Williamson Sylvester Stuckey. This has been confirmed by countless friends, business associates and family. Perhaps he saw them as ongoing extensions of himself, a connecting link between his ancestors, himself, and future generations. At any rate, he loved his grandchildren with an unabashed devotion, and took great pride in them. Eventually, he had seven grandchildren who knew him affectionately as "Big Daddy." Ethel Stuckey was called "Big Mama" and she shared Stuckey's love for all of them.

The first, Williamson Sylvester Stuckey, III, was born on July 3, 1958, to his son Billy Stuckey, Jr. and his then wife, Anne Armistead Stuckey. He was followed by Stuart Anne, on April 18, 1960. (Billy Stuckey and Anne Armistead were later divorced.)

The two oldest Stuckey grandchildren were followed by three children of Billy Stuckey and Ethelynn McMillan Stuckey: Scott Maloy, born on March 23, 1964; Ethel Stephanie on December 25, 1965, and Jay-Gould on April 17, 1968.

Lynda Stuckey Franklin and Dean Franklin gave Stuckey two grandchildren: Russell Dean Franklin, III, born on June 8, 1964, and Beverly Stuckey Franklin, born May 6, 1969. Thus, during the eleven-year period from 1958 to 1969, Stuckey and Ethel acquired seven grandchildren.

As Stuckey's oldest grandchild and namesake, young Billy was showered with attention from the very beginning. As he had done with his own children, Stuckey liked to take "Little Billy" around with him, even while he was still in diapers, for brief visits to his office and on errands about town.

Some of Billy Stuckey, III's very earliest memories include visits in Eastman with his grandparents. In the family he was known affectionately as "Little Billy" in order to distinguish him from his father. "I spent a lot of time in Eastman, even though I grew up in Augusta," said Billy, III. "Stuart (his sister) and I visited them real often. In the beginning, Big Daddy would send Boots over in his car to get us, and later on when he got a plane, he would send his pilot over for us. We felt very special and important."

"Big Mama was a very wise woman," her oldest grandson declared. "Big Daddy was a better person because of having her for his wife. She was always there for him, and she brought a new dimension to their life. Big Daddy was a complete person with her. I spent a lot of time riding with Big Daddy, looking at his farmland. He got a new Cadillac every year—later on, I think that Pet gave him a new one every year," Billy III said.

When Billy III was old enough to drive, he frequently went by himself to Eastman to visit his grandparents when Stuart could not go. "Big Daddy loved to visit the Stuckey stores in Florida, and also the one at Folkston. I would go along many times, just to ride with him," young Billy recalled. "Sometimes he would fly down to St. Simons, then get in his Cadillac and drive all around to the stores. He would get out his chewing tobacco and his spittoon and he would hit the road. He always dressed real nice, but when he got in his car, he would get comfortable by loosening his belt. He drove himself a lot, even when Boots was along. Sometimes Boots would ride in the front seat with him and I would be in the back. Big Mama would not let Boots drive her, though. She liked to drive herself."

Billy III remembers that his grandfather often took him for haircuts when he was in Eastman. "The barber, Mr. Pruett, was two doors down the street," he recalls, "and I guess he cut Big Daddy's hair, too."

In turning his thoughts backward, he reminisced, "If I were to use one word to describe Big Daddy, it would be 'dynamic.' He had a good sense of humor, smiled a lot and liked to hang out with his buddies and play cards."

Billy III remembers, "Big Daddy's office after Pet took over was something to see. Elva Lee's office (Elva Lee Connell, Stuckey's secretary) was one flight up, then you went down a flight to his big, impressive office, with a board room next to it." As to Stuckey's candy, though, he did not just "feed" it to his grandchildren. "Maybe because it was so available, we just did not eat a lot of it," his grandson recalls. "I did like pecan clusters and chocolate candy, though."

In later years, Stuckey's oldest grandson, like so many other people, remembered Stuckey's love for his rocking chair in the lobby of the Stuckey Timberland offices in the heart of Eastman. "I would sit with him and Boots would be with us, too," he recalls. "He would talk to everybody—anybody he could—about almost anything."

As the oldest grandchild, Billy III was eighteen years old when his grandfather died in 1977. "Really I was on toward being nineteen," he said. Thus, he remembers Stuckey quite well and in a different manner, perhaps, than do the younger grandchildren.

Stuart Anne Stuckey also grew up in Augusta. Like her brother, she spent a great deal of time in Eastman, and she got to know and love her grandparents quite well. She remembers, "Big Daddy would send Boots to get Billy and me on Friday afternoon when we got out of school. We spent weekends in Eastman real often, and we would have Christmas in Augusta, then go to Eastman for part of the holidays. Or we would go to Eastman and then on to St. Simons Island."

Stuart said, "Almost all the Christmases and New Years that I can remember were spent at St. Simons."

Stuart recalls, "Big Daddy was very good with children. He treated me with dignity and would listen to my opinions, while most adults do not do this. Then he might give me a different opinion, though, but he certainly did not believe that a child should be seen and not heard. He had a respect for children and for everyone."

She reminisced, "Big Daddy was a man with an enormous heart. I have fond memories of him—he was so special to me. Every day now I remember lessons that he taught me, although I did not know he was teaching me at the time. For example, I will find it easy to make a decision on some issue. Then I look back and know that it was because of how Big Daddy handled things that I know what to do. I find myself thinking, 'Now, what would Big Daddy do in this?' And I know what to do."

She continued, "He loved people. He loved to sit on the pier at St. Simons and talk to people. He could talk half a day to someone he did not even know, and I would be content to listen. He had a real rapport with people. He would talk about farm equipment, tractors, or whatever, and he always had me along, but I was never bored. He would always take the time to explain things to me."

In 1977 when Stuckey died, Stuart was seventeen. "His death was devastating to me," she declared. "We were so close, and I missed him so much. He would call me all the time, not just on special occasions, just for no reason at all but just to chat. He was interested in the smallest details of my life. We had a sort of ritual—he would not really say 'I love you' but he would end our conversation with, 'Bye, I love.' And I would say the same thing. I am not sure whether this was our own private ritual. He may have done the same thing with the other grandchildren." (This was a special ritual that Stuckey had only with Stuart.)

Ethel Stephanie Stuckey was much younger than her older siblings, Billy III, and Stuart Anne, her half-brother and half-sister. She was born on December 25, 1965, in Eastman, the daughter of Billy Stuckey, Jr. and Ethelynn McMillan Stuckey. She grew up in Washington, where her father was a United States Congressman, but visited Eastman often, particularly on holidays and special occasions. She is the namesake of her grandmother, Ethel Stuckey.

"I remember one story about Big Daddy particularly," Stephanie said. "It was on my birthday which is on Christmas day, and I think I was eight years old. After all the Christmas presents had been opened, Big Daddy took me aside and told me he had a birthday present for me. He said I could choose between two presents. He showed me five twenty-dollar bills, but said I could also have X amount of Pet stock," she remembered. "Of course, I said I wanted the money. He just looked at me and said, 'Honey, you are a damn fool.' So I got the stock and did not get to choose after all. Of course, now I understand and I am glad he gave me the stock."

Beverly Stuckey Franklin, the youngest of the Stuckey grandchildren, grew up in Eastman and spent a great deal of time with her grandparents. Because Stuckey was retired during her early years and thus had a great deal of time on his hands, Beverly remembers his spending much time with her.

"Big Daddy never treated me like a child," Beverly recalls. "He was more of a buddy than a grandparent. I used to spend every weekend with him and Big Mama. I would be sleeping with him and he would hear a thud—he had pushed me off the bed. He would say, 'Beverly, are you okay?' And I would say, 'Yes, sir.' He would say, 'Get back in the bed then.'"

"Big Daddy was, in a way, strict, but I always knew how to get what I wanted. He simply could not stand the sight of blood. Once when I was visiting and Big Mama was gone, I ran into a brick wall and started bleeding profusely. He got Boots and they took me to the emergency room at the hospital. I was frightened really more than hurt, and they had to strap me down to take some stitches. I was kicking and screaming and the doctor told Big Daddy he would have to do something to keep me still. Big Daddy took out a ten dollar bill and leaned over and whispered to me that I could have it if I would be quiet. He tucked it into the strap that was holding me down. He said it to me real low so no one else could hear it. I got quiet immediately and the doctor fixed me up. I still have the scar on my forehead today." She lifted her dark bangs to show the small scar.

"Big Daddy was really a pushover. He and five or six people would be playing cards on the weekend when I was there—and they would be placing bets. He would let some change accidentally fall under the table where I would be playing, and I would get it. Only he and I would know about it—it was our secret."

He was really a "people person," she said. "The people who worked for him were not treated like employees but like friends. They were part of the company—he treated them as though they were important, as they indeed were."

One of the family's favorite stories about Beverly is one which she herself remembers, although she was very young. "Or it may be that I have heard it so often that I think I remember." One Sunday night Beverly was at her grandparents' home when her Big Daddy decided that he wanted a bacon, lettuce, and tomato sandwich for supper. Ethel did not have any tomatoes, so Stuckey took Beverly with him to a convenience store to buy tomatoes. Beverly, a toddler, was still in diapers, and she sat in her favorite spot—the arm rest in the front seat.

Stuckey left her in the car while he went in the store to buy the tomatoes. But he ran into a friend and chatted awhile, as was his custom. Meanwhile, Beverly, left to her own devices, locked the car door. The keys, of course, were in the ignition, and by then Beverly was under the steering wheel. Stuckey begged and tried to persuade Beverly to unlock the door, but she did not understand. She just looked at him and cried. He kept saying, "Push that button, Beverly." Finally, he went into the store and got a lollipop, showed it to her, and she immediately unlocked the door. As Stuckey was getting into the car, however, he discovered that the seat was very wet. Beverly had not only locked him out of his car, but she had also wet the driver's seat. After that, Stuckey was more careful and did not leave Beverly alone in the car.

Beverly recalls fondly, "Big Daddy would call me his 'sidekick.' He would drive up to our house in his big yellow Cadillac, blowing the horn, and I would run out of the house, ready to go wherever he was going. My mother had some problems with this—he would not tell her where we were going or how long we would be gone. But I was never bored with him—he was so much fun. He would put his spittoon on the far right side of the car. It was amazing to see how far he could spit tobacco juice. I remember that he had spittoons at his house and in the office, too. I admired his spitting so much that one time I asked, 'Big Daddy, can I chew some tobacco, too?' He gave me a small piece, and it made me so sick that I never wanted any chewing tobacco again."

She recalls that Stuckey liked to lie on the couch with his head on his big green pillow while he watched Jeopardy on television. "I remember this so well," she said. "He would lie there and drink Old Crow—he could have afforded anything he wanted in the world to drink—but he drank Old Crow. He was completely unpretentious, although he liked to make money. But it was not the money itself that was really important—it was people. He was completely unimpressed with the money he made, and success never went to his head. I was too young really to know about the business then. I just knew him as a warm, loving grandfather who treated me in a special way. I think that I was one of his favorite grandchildren, perhaps because of circumstances. I was there in Eastman at a time when he had retired and had time to devote to me. I knew that I was special."

She remembers accompanying her grandfather to the candy plant. "I could have all the candy I wanted to eat," she recalls, "but after I'd eaten two pecan logs or so, they weren't so enticing any more. It was always exciting to be with him and to see the candy being made. I loved divinity and chocolate covered coconut candy best." Beverly remembers Emily, the parrot at the Eastman Stuckey store, very well. She also remembers that the store had a horse that cost a dime to ride.

"You know, it sounds contradictory to describe Big Mama as a Southern lady—which she certainly was—and in the next breath to say that she loved to play poker. But it was true. She was great at poker playing." When Beverly visited her grandparents, she recalls eating deviled ham and Ritz crackers. "Also Big Mama would have steak and grits—the steak would be cooked in the gravy and stirred into the grits. I loved it and so did they," Beverly reminisced. "When you ate at their house, it was pure country. It was 'down home' all the way," she chuckled. Vera, the cook who worked for Ethel Stuckey many years, served Beverly a special drink of sugar, vanilla and milk. "I was such a skinny little kid. I guess she thought I needed this, " Beverly said.

Beverly's eyes grew misty as she reflected, "Big Daddy was a Southern gentlemen—he was the very epitome of the quintessential gentleman. I loved him so much and he was so important to me. I was only seven years old when he died, but he influenced me so much. His influence is still very strong in our family today. Everything we do is influenced by him and his life. He is still very much with us."

Beverly had one final reflection. "The last time I saw Big Daddy alive, Jimmy Carter had been elected president. He gave me a ballpoint pen with clear liquid and a peanut in it. When I left him that day, I said as I always did, 'I love you, Big Daddy.'"

Russell Dean Franklin, III (Russ) also grew up in Eastman. Thus, he was near his Big Daddy and Big Mama Stuckey and spent a great deal of time with them. He also spent much time with his Franklin grandparents who lived in Eastman. As Russ grew older—about the time he was six years old or so—Stuckey retired, and during this period he had a great deal more time to spend with his grandchildren. Apparently, Stuckey liked to take one grandchild at the time around with him, because Russ, as do the others, remembers riding around alone with his grandfather to look at his farmland and timberland. This explains why each grandchild felt that he or she was Stuckey's favorite.

Russ, however, has a special memory. "I would go with Big Daddy to his pig farm—it was between Eastman and Cochran, and I remember looking at the huge hogs and being offended by their smell. He would tell me that it was the smell of money," Russ recalls. "Big Daddy always drove a Cadillac and he would not hesitate to take off across a field or down a little trail in it," Russ recalls. "He would go anywhere, no matter how rough the road." Russ was a Davy Crockett fan, and recalls that on a trip with his grandparents to North Carolina, "Big Daddy bought me a coon skin hat."

Chapter 12

YEARS OF CHANGE

By 1964 the Stuckey stores numbered 160, located primarily in the Southeast. Business was good and growth was continuing, but Stuckey, although still a relatively young man, had developed some troubling health problems which may or may not have influenced his decision to consider the sale of his business. He did not dwell on his health condition, however, and, in fact, some close friends and business associates were unaware of it, according to their recollections.

Many persons close to Stuckey believed he was watching closely the changes that were occurring which would have a strong impact on his business—fast foods were gaining a popular foothold, and convenience stores were becoming increasingly popular. He knew these would gain a large share of the market, and that the customer base was changing. He was first, last and always a pragmatist. Others, however, note that flexibility was one of Stuckey's strongest characteristics and many believe that he would have adjusted to whatever changes occurred.

Billy Stuckey, in reflecting upon the course taken by his father, recalls the circumstances this way: "He got frustrated—he had some health problems, but he was still a young man. At the time I did not understand it. He may have started thinking—was the concept (of Stuckey's) good, would it last forever? I negotiated the final settlement with Pet Milk Company, at Dad's instructions. They (Pet) came along and had been acquiring a group of companies, and Stuckey's was one of the companies Pet was looking at, but Dad had some other feelers out himself. Looking back, I think that part of it was that he was just curious about what it was worth.

"My recollection was that he was flabbergasted at what they offered him. He had told me privately one amount he would take, and Pet's first offer was far above this. Then Dad figured—if this is the first offer, it is not their final one. Being the trader he was, he was intrigued. When they offered him more than he expected, he said, look, go back and see if they will give me X amount. So I went back to New Orleans and negotiated. We had gotten the price up a couple of times, and every time, he would think they gave in too easily. The truth is that he merged with Pet, rather than sold. He felt the company was going places. I think we were probably the largest family shareholders, although it was only five, six or seven percent (of the company). I went back down to New Orleans and kept negotiating—and that last time I came back and it was basically what he wanted. It freed him from having to run a business."

In looking back at the merger from the perspective of more than three decades, Billy Stuckey said, "To be truthful, the management of Stuckey's was really pretty thin. It was mainly my father and Russell Franklin, and Mr. Franklin had already left the company. I was there, but my God, I didn't have any kind of seasoning or any real experience, although I thought I was pretty sharp. Hell, I was at the learning stage." At any rate, Stuckey decided to go ahead with the deal, and the merger with Pet, Inc. took place on December 14, 1964.

Looking back, Billy believes his father had thought the situation through very carefully. "He was concerned about at what point he was going to reach the saturation point with his stores on the interstate. At that time, they were located about every fifty miles or so apart. He wondered where he could expand to, and in a way he was right, because we had tried a couple of times, unsuccessfully, off the interstate. Pet had the capital to open new stores all over the country."

Stuckey's fears about how the interstates would eventually affect his business proved unfounded. He had plenty of stores on the interstate, and traffic was heavier than it had been on the two-lane highways. However, both I-16 and I-75 bypassed Eastman, as he was quick to point out. Although not generally publicized at the time, the exact amount of the sale was speculated upon, both in the media and by many persons, and it was often under-estimated.

As part of the merger, Stuckey became a vice president and member of the board of the Pet Inc., while remaining president of the Stuckey's Division within the Pet Corporation. Stuckey managed his company until 1970 when he requested early retirement. During the six-year period that Stuckey remained as president of the Stuckey division, (1964-70) Stuckey stores grew from 160 to 350. The Pet Corporation had set an expansion goal of 25 to 30 new stores per year, and this exceeded the goal.

The frequently asked question of whether Stuckey ever regretted selling to Pet brings various answers from those who knew him best. "Oh, every time he would get mad at something Pet did, he would probably regret it," his son declares. "He did a lot of 'mully-grubbing'. But over the long haul, no, I do not think that he regretted the decision. It was a good deal, and at first he was active and had a seat on the board, and when they did something he did not like, he would let them know it. He had authority. The board seat was important, and he was very vocal and in charge. That was his nature. His influence was there. When he stepped down (in 1970) he was not as happy. He needed to be busy all the time."

It was hard for Stuckey to be a second lieutenant when he had been a general all of his life. His mind was not geared to the rocking chair. After the merger, there was a contingency period from 1964 through 1967. Ted Gamble, president of Pet, had worked very closely with Stuckey on details of the merger, and the two men communicated very well and were able to work out various details amicably.

But in 1966 Gamble died suddenly, and the management of Stuckey's began to change also. The basic philosophy set up by Stuckey began to change, and this was very disturbing to him. He had no real control over the situation. As a close associate said, "Stuckey loved to work and to run things. He was a man who did not like Saturday because it was not a work day."

In general, the deal with Pet was more complicated because of the involvement of various family members in the Stuckey operation. Basically the merger provided for Pet to buy the candy factory, the right to expand Stuckey's by building new stores, and the gasoline deal with Texaco. At this point, Pet did not receive any of the stores already in existence. These stores were managed by Stuckey Stores, Inc. which was, in turn, owned by Billy Stuckey. Pet supplied all the candy and gasoline to all the Stuckey stores in the country, and this resulted in a healthy split of profits between Pet and the Stuckey operation. And at this point, Stuckey was in position to have a hand in the management of the old stores, through his son's operation, and in the building of new stores because he was a chief executive officer of Pet.

Jack Lott, who had worked for Stuckey from 1954 onward, said that when the merger with Pet took place, Pet got a large percentage of Stuckey Timberland, plus Stuckey Investments and Stuckey Pecan Company. However, after a certain length of time, Pet agreed to sell the Stuckey Timberland property back to the family. Lott believes that Pet met all of its commitments of the merger. After the merger, Pet built a new two-story building for Stuckey's which was about three times the size of the previous building.

Elva Lee Connell remembers her own pleasure with having large and beautifully decorated offices with traditional furnishings. "Important people were visiting Mr. Stuckey all the time," she recalls. "He was involved with the stock market, and things were always busy and hectic. A visitor once said to me, 'This place is busier than Wall Street.' Those early days, after the merger with Pet, were exciting times."

Stuckey brought in James Spradley from Atlanta to learn the business and then he took over as president in 1970, about five years after Stuckey sold to Pet, when Stuckey announced his retirement as president of the Stuckey Division. On his last day as CEO, there was a gala open house at the Eastman company headquarters. Sadly, he found retirement was a burden, too, albeit a different type.

Spradley served as the bridge between the Stuckey family and the new company, a not very enviable position. One of the circumstances he had to deal with was the oil embargo in 1973 which greatly affected travel and tourism. Gasoline prices soared and fewer Americans went on long vacations, so they needed fewer rest stops at Stuckey stores. Most people stayed close to home. Even those who traveled less had more choices available. Texaco's full-service products ran high compared to self-service gasoline pumps which were becoming the rage. Fast food establishments were a dime a dozen on the interstate, and places such as Starvin' Marvin offered self-service gasoline, too, along with groceries and sundries. It was fast becoming a new and different world.

Changes began to take place in the Stuckey Division, and they continued over a seven-year period. The new management of Pet expanded the stores all over the country, from 160 to 350. Stuckey stores were located as far away as California to the West, and as far as Vermont to the North. People in Eastman who had owned stores a long time began to lose money, and they would express their dissatisfaction and concerns to Stuckey, their longtime friend and mentor. Although he was powerless to help them, he felt their burden, nevertheless, and he was greatly troubled. As a result of these changes, Lynda Stuckey Franklin and her husband, Dean Franklin, started a chain of stores called Wayfara.

By now the political bug had bitten Billy, even as it had his father, and in 1966 he ran for a seat in the United States House of Representatives as a Congressman for the Eighth District.

About his entry into politics, Billy commented, "Dad did not think I had much of a chance of getting elected when I first ran for Congress. I did not have enough sense to know that you don't run against an incumbent, and so I ran, despite the fact that at that time only four or five percent of incumbents were defeated. Once I was running, though, Dad got behind me. He was something else when he got geared up and going. Although it would take me away from the business, he was behind me and I could not have run successfully without my father's help."

Billy went on to say, "The strongest vote I ever got was in Dodge County—all due to my father's influence. In general, he was well liked in Eastman, but there were some detractors. He managed to stir up and inflame some people because of his politics." In 1966 Bill Stuckey, Jr. was elected to Congress, representing the Eighth District of Georgia, and serving five terms, from 1967 to 1976. The Eighth District of Georgia includes twenty-four counties: Appling, Atkinson, Bacon, Ben Hill, Berrien, Bleckley, Brantley, Camden, Charlton, Clinch, Coffee, Cook, Dodge, Echols, Glynn, Irwin, Jeff Davis, Lanier, Lowndes, Pierce, Telfair, Ware, Wayne and Wilcox, with a population in 1970 of 350,929.

"My father's unusual rapport with blacks was a bonus for me when I ran for Congress," the former Congressman recalls. "Various black groups would tell me they were supporting me, and I finally realized that it was my father's influence that got me this support. They (blacks) would tell me they had to plan their trips back in the '40s and '50s when they were going across the country so they could use the rest rooms at Stuckey stores. In those pre-integration days, public rest rooms were off-limits to blacks, but Stuckey's was different, said to be the only stores in the south where blacks could use the rest rooms."

Billy moved to Washington, and sold Stuckey Stores, Inc. to Pet. Although he retained part ownership of several stores, this gave Pet its first opportunity to own any of the stores begun by the founder. This brought a whole new perspective to the operation.

In looking back on this period later, Stuckey openly admitted to differences of opinion with Pet on the way that business was handled. He said in an interview, "The company isn't like it was when I operated it. I affectionately referred to the Stuckey business method as taking a bunch of good country boys and training them, giving them interests in the stores and then watching them do the finest job you've ever seen. To me, the franchisees were one of the most important parts of my business, and I looked after them. Pet does not do that—they are more interested in making money for themselves."

One of the changes resulting from the sale to Pet was that Stuckey's longtime friend and the company's first executive, Russell D. Franklin, left the business. "I objected to the sale—I wanted to buy it (the business)," Franklin recalls. "Stuckey was never really happy about the business after the sale," Franklin believes. "He was no longer in charge. He would sometimes call me and we would get together and talk. He was often angry."

Franklin remembers that Stuckey seemed to be in fairly good health at the time of the sale. He believes that Stuckey's main reason for selling was that he wanted to distribute his assets to his heirs without being taxed. He got a tremendous price for Stuckey's, and the stock transfer was a non-taxable deal.

Senator Hugh Gillis of Soperton, Stuckey's friend since Legislature days in the late 1950s, said, "I never did really ask him why he sold out. He was not in good health, I know. I guess he figured that he had gone as far as he could go with the business, and I am sure that he thought Pet Milk would do a good job in managing it. He trusted Ted Gamble and had a good relationship with him. But it was not the same after that—he was not close to Pet after Gamble died, and the relationship kind of dwindled or soured. After a few years, IC Industries bought out Stuckey's from Pet and it went further downhill. The business relationship was nothing compared to when Stuckey was in charge."

Emmett Barnes, Macon real estate developer and entrepreneur, commented, "After he sold to Pet, though, he did not have as much authority—I think once it was sold, he was a different person. He did not have the challenges but he never lost sight of his friends. He still had his parties down at St. Simons."

Duck Moody, Macon banker (now deceased), recalled, "A few weeks after the deal with Pet was consummated, Stuckey had the Board of Directors of Pet to meet in Eastman, and we had a big cookout. Mr. Latiner, whose family started Pet, was there, and so was Ted Gamble, the president of Pet. Then the next year Stuckey had a big party at St. Simons. When Gamble died, the company and its policy made a distinct change. And Stuckey came off their board. He did not agree with the politics of the new president. It was under him that IC Industries got control of Pet some years later."

Moody recalls that "Stuckey got tired of fooling with it and decided he would step down as CEO of the Stuckey division of Pet, and it was turned over to Jim Spradley. But the company did not fare well after Stuckey pulled out. He was the guiding light."

Meanwhile, the war in Vietnam was under way, beginning in the mid '60s and carrying over into the early '70s. Demonstrations against the war were held across the country—an example was the 50,000 persons who demonstrated in 1967 at the Lincoln Memorial in Washington, D.C., and student demonstrations were common across the country. American soldiers were fighting and dying in jungles in this faraway land, and those who survived would not only be denied a hero's welcome, but would be actually derided. In 1973 the strange war came to a close when a cease fire was signed, but some fighting would continue, and there was no clear victor.

In 1968 another tragedy struck the star-crossed Kennedy family. Senator Robert F. Kennedy, John F. Kennedy's brother, a candidate for the presidency, was assassinated in Los Angeles, and civil rights leader Martin Luther King, Jr. was assassinated in Memphis, Tennessee. That same year Richard M. Nixon became the 37th president of the United States, and the Republican party was back in power. Achievements in space continued, and by 1969 the United States had landed a man on the moon. Further space explorations continued, some in cooperation with the Soviets.

The economy was in trouble. In 1970 the Dow-Jones average dropped to 631. By 1971 President Nixon found it necessary to impose a ninety-day freeze on wages and prices, a measure designed to curb inflation and strengthen the United States' balance of payments position. But in 1972 the Dow Jones recovered and managed to close for the first time above 1,000. Nixon was reelected in 1972, but hard days were ahead for him and the country. Media reports about the Watergate Conspiracy were building, and in 1973 five original defendants pled guilty before Judge John J. Sirica. The country was transfixed with the televised hearings headed by the Senate Watergate Committee Chairman Sam Ervin, Jr. The House Judiciary Committee recommended three articles of impeachment for consideration by the full House of Representatives in connection with the alleged cover-up. Eventually, on August 9, 1974, Nixon resigned, and Gerald Ford became the 38th president.

Needless to say, Stuckey, in his retirement, followed very closely the developments on the national political scene, and spent much time discussing the implications of these happenings. The energy crisis greatly affected the tourist trade, and all travel suffered. Another mode of travel by foot, which required energy of another sort, called "streaking," swept college campuses, and provided its own brand of comic relief as college students stripped off their clothing and "streaked" by running fast in populated sections. The real energy crisis would continue into the late 1970s, affecting tourist trade and troubling businesses which depended upon it.

In 1976 the country turned its thoughts toward the past and its beginnings, and celebrated the Bicentennial with great enthusiasm. The sight of tall ships from 31 nations parading up the Hudson River, whether viewed in person or via television, was a never-to-be-forgotten experience.

And Stuckey, ever the staunch Democrat, was pleased when a man from Georgia, James Earl Carter, Jr., became the 39th President of the United States. Carter, who hailed from nearby Plains, was elected in 1976 and took office in 1977. The Democrats were back in power.

Charles Eckles (now deceased), an accountant at Stuckey's, recalled, "Stuckey was at loose ends (in the later years). He never did talk to me about the sale to Pet, though. I think Stuckey felt like trading out and getting the stock would be good security for his family. He felt that if something happened to him, nobody in the family would take over. By then, having all this stock, they would be secure. In later years, Billy decided to get back involved in the business. But things had changed by then, and the economy had changed by the time Billy decided to get back into the business. But for this, I don't think that Stuckey would have sold to Pet. Later on, if he had it to do over, I don't think Stuckey would have sold out."

Almost everyone agreed, including the Stuckey family, that things were never the same after the company was sold. Billy Stuckey said, "Instead of marketing what worked, Pet wanted to look good on Wall Street and let the company-owned stores go to hell in order to keep the bottom line up." According to published reports at the time, a spokesman for Pet, however, said that the problem was a changing world that included McDonald's, Hardee's, Shoney's and gas stations that sold food and novelties.

In 1976 Billy Stuckey, after having served five terms, decided not to offer for re-election to Congress, and began to focus on the family's various businesses.

As though working under a premonition, Stuckey had begun to get all his affairs in order in 1976, Elva Lee Connell, his secretary, remembers. "It was uncanny, as we looked back on it," she said. On January 6, 1977, he worked throughout the morning in the office, and went home at lunchtime, as was his custom. When he returned from lunch, Elva Lee noticed a small spot of blood at the corner of his mouth. When she called this to Stuckey's attention, he dismissed it by saying it was from dental work that he had recently had. Looking back, she considers it a danger signal. That night Stuckey had a cerebral hemorrhage and died in the Eastman Hospital.

Billy was in Washington, D.C., taking care of family business at his father's direction, when he received a telephone call that day from his father, asking him to return home, without any explanation as to why he needed him. He left immediately and was enroute from Washington, D.C. to Eastman when his father died.

The sad news shocked Eastman and Dodge County citizens, as well as countless numbers of Stuckey's friends and business associates across the country. Stuckey's funeral service, conducted by his longtime friend, the Rev. J.B. (Jake) Hutchinson, in the Eastman United Methodist Church, drew an overflowing crowd of mourners from all walks of life and from great distances. It was one of the largest, if not the largest, funeral ever held in Eastman. His body was interred in the Woodlawn Cemetery.

"I got to his funeral a half hour early," said Emmett Barnes. "I had to sit on the back pew. The church was filled and many people had to stand outside. This is a testimony to how much people thought of Stuckey." A woman who worked in the candy plant expressed succinctly the feelings of countless people, "We'll never see the likes of Stuckey again."

Chapter 13

EPILOGUE
AFTER JANUARY 7, 1977

In 1978, following Stuckey's death in 1977, more problems surfaced when Pet was bought by Illinois Central Industries, a Chicago conglomerate. Pet fought the merger and lost. Stuckey officials began to close company-owned stores across the country.

Frank Stuckey, Stuckey's half brother, who was also involved in the business, commented in 1984 to a *Houston Chronicle* columnist, "The sonic booms we hear around here every afternoon are not jets, but my brother turning over in his grave in disgust over what these corporate jerks have done to his company." Stuckey's son said in the same interview, "My father probably is haunting the hell out of them (Pet officials) for ruining his company."

In 1981 Stuckey headquarters moved from Eastman to Atlanta. Spradley retired as president at the same time. An article in *The Atlanta Journal-Constitution Magazine* was entitled "Will Stuckey's Lose Its Flavor in the City?" The article recapped the events which led up to the move, along with a history of the company's founding.

Today the former Stuckey's, Inc. building and candy plant, where the Stuckey dream was incubated and launched, is owned by Standard Candy Company and they have a contract to supply candy products to the remaining approximately 100 Stuckey stores.

The Stuckey Timberland Corporation has prospered far beyond Stuckey's wildest dream. Stuckey had no way of knowing what a "sleeping giant" timber was; nor did anyone else in those days. Andy Stone of Eastman is president of Stuckey Timberland, Billy Stuckey is chairman of the board, and Lynda Stuckey Franklin is co-chairman. Today, Stuckey Timberland owns approximately 33,000 acres of timberland.

On May 1, 1985, Billy Stuckey bought Stuckey's Corporation from Illinois Central Industries, Inc., ending seventeen years during which the company was not owned by Stuckey family members. The company made arrangements with Standard Company of Nashville to produce candy with the Stuckey's name.

Following Stuckey's death on January 6, 1977, Ethel continued to live in the family home in the heart of Eastman, and the old Victorian house with its gingerbread trim remained the center of family activities. Despite obvious changes in her life and the fact that she missed her husband of more than 45 years terribly, she carried on and continued with her many social activities. She was a member of the William Few Chapter of the Daughters of the American Revolution, and was a member of the Eastman First United Methodist Church and the Alathean Sunday School Class.

After several years, Ethel's health began to decline. In spite of a laryngectomy, her activities were not limited and she remained active and enjoyed visits from her family and friends. Her grandchildren brought particular pleasure to her. Because she could no longer speak easily on the telephone, her children, Lynda and Billy, had a facsimile machine installed in her living room. She enjoyed regular "instant" letters which her family faxed to her, and she marveled at the immediacy of the communication. When visited in her home in October 1990, Ethel Stuckey showed photographs of her grandchildren and boasted of their accomplishments.

Ethel Mullis Stuckey died on March 27, 1991, in Eastman, and her body was interred in Woodlawn Cemetery, her husband's final resting place. The mausoleum bears the familiar Stuckey logo, a stark reminder to all who view it of the impact this man and woman, Williamson Sylvester Stuckey and Ethel Mullis Stuckey, had upon the face of Eastman, Georgia, and indeed upon the state, the region, and the country.

Today Williamson Sylvester (Billy) Stuckey, Jr. lives in Washington, D.C., with his wife, Ethelynn McMillan Stuckey, but he maintains close ties with Eastman and Dodge County. He has a small, neatly kept farmhouse on a lake, located on the Stuckey farm near Eastman, and happily spends much leisure time there. He returns regularly to Eastman for Stuckey Timberland Inc. meetings and to take care of family business. He has an office in the Stuckey Timberland Building in Eastman, and offices in Washington.

Lynda Stuckey Franklin and her husband, Russell Dean Franklin, Jr., today live in their home on Sea Island, Georgia. However, they keep a home in Eastman to which they return often. Dean's father, Russell Dean Franklin and his wife, Sallie, live in Eastman. Lynda comes to Eastman regularly for board meetings of Stuckey Timberland. She maintains an office also in the Stuckey Building, and she has an office in a building near the family home in the heart of Eastman, as well as an office at St. Simons Island.

Boots Fluellen was deeply grieved after Stuckey's death, and was never quite the same again. Lynda Stuckey describes Boots as being completely "devastated" following her father's death. But he continued to serve Ethel Stuckey and the family. He remained on the payroll and always ate breakfast and lunch at the Stuckey table. In recognition and appreciation of his loyal service, Ethel Stuckey bought a comfortable, air-conditioned home for him and his family.

When Boots' health began to fail, he would sometimes obstinately refuse to go to see a doctor. His wife or one of his children would telephone Ethel Stuckey and tell her about it.

Ethel would simply tell him, "Boots, you know you need to go to the doctor, and I want you to do it." Boots would say, "All right, Missus." And he would do what she asked. Lynda remembers that Boots was a "good person." She said, however, "Daddy would get mad with him sometimes, just like family. It would not last, though. Boots was Daddy's right arm. Boots was a real character, though." Boots died in Eastman on April 17, 1990, about a year before Ethel Stuckey's death.

Billy III was graduated from Augusta College with a major in history. Today he lives in Augusta where he has business interests ranging from billboard rentals to consumer finance companies. He is married to Catherine Clayton Stuckey, and they have two children: Marietta Bryson, born December 5, 1991, and Williamson Sylvester Stuckey, IV, born October 25, 1995. Catherine is merchandise representative for the Georgia State Lottery.

Stuart Anne Stuckey and her two sons live in Eastman in the family home of Billy and Ethelynn Stuckey which she is renovating. James Austin Putnam, Stuart's older boy, was born on June 26, 1983, and the younger, Williamson Elliott Putnam, was born on June 24, 1987.

Ethel Stephanie Stuckey—the namesake of her grandmother, Ethel, attended Vanderbilt University and spent a year abroad in Aix-en-Provence, France. She earned her law degree in 1992 at the University of Georgia Law School where she was president of her class. She now lives and practices law in Atlanta. On May 25, 1996, (her father's birthday) she was married in Washington, D.C. to Gerald Richard Weber. Gerry Weber is the legal director of the Georgia A.C.L.U. Stephanie, following in her father's and grandfather's footsteps, is actively involved in Georgia politics. She was elected as a delegate to the 1988 and the 1996 Democratic National Conventions, and she serves on a variety of state boards and committees, including the Georgia Commission on Women and the Jeanette Rankin Foundation.

Russell Dean (Russ) Franklin, III, was graduated from Mercer University in 1988 and obtained his master's degree in English from Florida State University in 1992. He taught high school English in Monroe, Georgia, for one year. In 1993 he was accepted into the Ph.D. program at Florida State University in the field of English with a focus on creative writing.

Russ has had numerous works published while he continued to work on his Ph.D. He also taught Freshman English at Florida State University. He married Amy Elizabeth McBride on June 19, 1993, in Clearwater, Florida. Amy obtained her master's degree in elementary education in 1996, and is teaching third grade in Tallahassee, Florida. Russ and Amy expect the birth of their first child in September 1997.

Beverly Stuckey Franklin, the youngest of Stuckey's grandchildren, was graduated from Mercer University in 1991 with a bachelor of arts degree in English with a minor in religion and concentration in classical studies. After working in the family business and spending a year in Alaska, Beverly is pursuing a master's degree in elementary education at Mercer University.

Scott Maloy Stuckey studied film and video in Chillicothe, Ohio, and Orlando, Florida. For several years, he owned a recording studio, Sound Gallery, in Athens, Georgia, where he worked with REM and Vic Chestnut, and others. Scott is the father of two daughters, Christine Marie Stuckey, born May 31, 1985, and Michelle Stephanie Stuckey, born September 20, 1988. On August 10, 1991, Scott married Kristina Louise Johnson in Athens, Georgia. Currently, they live in Austin, Texas, where he continues his career in film and video, and where Kristina works as an information specialist for the University of Texas.

Jay-Gould Williamson Stuckey graduated magna cum laude from Brown University in 1990 with a major in studio art, and was named to membership in Phi Beta Kappa. For the next two years he taught art at St. Patrick's Episcopal Day School in Washington, D.C. In 1994, he entered the graduate program at the Chicago Art Institute, where he received his M.F.A. degree in 1996.

During the years from college graduation to the present, Jay-Gould has had art exhibitions in New York City, Atlanta, Chicago, and Washington, D.C. He moved to Los Angeles in the fall of 1996, to continue his career in art and teaching.

Thus, there are now six great-grandchildren, none of whom Stuckey got to know. They were all born after his death, but Ethel had great pride and interest in the great-grandchildren.

W. Frank Stuckey, Stuckey's half-brother, has retired and today lives with his wife, Ann Reagin Stuckey, in their home north of Eastman. Felix Stuckey, his brother, died April 17, 1989, in Dodge County, and he is buried in the historic Orphans Cemetery. Felix's widow, Wilma Winifred Carter Stuckey, died in 1994.

Today the Stuckey legend lives on, and there remains a certain mystique about the Stuckey name. For example, in early July, 1992, Pat Sajak, Wheel of Fortune emcee on CBS, in interviewing a contestant for the game show, was trying to place the location of the contestant's hometown in Illinois. After she had explained where it was, Sajak concluded with, "Oh, yes, now I know. And isn't there a Stuckey's up the road?" Similar references are regularly made on various television shows.

Indeed there might well be a Stuckey's "up the road a piece" almost anywhere today, although the likelihood of the presence of a Stuckey's is not so great today as when the chain was in its heyday. In late 1996 there are around 100 Stuckey stores operating across the country.

The new 5400 square-foot Stuckey Timberland, Inc. building, designed in the Williamsburg style by architect Mark Studstill, was dedicated on July 15, 1995. The firm of Graham and Studstill was the general contractor, and the interior design was done by Bill Brown of Brown Interiors in Dublin, Georgia. Fabrics and wall coverings are reproductions of those used in the restoration of the Williamsburg Colony buildings.

The handsome structure is located at 925 Hawkinsville Highway in Eastman, Georgia.

In the board room or conference room of the new building, a large portrait of Stuckey hangs on the wall. There is a strong feeling that, from this vantage point, he keeps a watchful eye on the decisions made here. Those who attend meetings around the large conference table find themselves looking frequently at the man in the portrait.

Because a country boy by the name of Williamson Sylvester Stuckey parlayed $35 into a multi-million dollar business, the lives of countless persons were forever changed. The little roadside stand in Eastman, Georgia grew up, and the lowly pecan gained new respect because Stuckey dared to pursue his dream.

Bibliography and Sources

Personal interviews, tape-recorded:

Elva Lee Connell, Eastman, Georgia—October 2, 1990, January 29, 1991, and October 15, 1992

Mrs. Verna Lee Ragan, Eastman, Georgia—June 17, 1991

Russell Franklin, Eastman, Georgia—July 24, 1991

Jack Lott, Eastman, Georgia—August 14, 1991

Frank Stuckey, Eastman, Georgia—August 14, 1991 and July 13, 1993

W. T. (Duck) Moody, Macon, Georgia—August 22, 1991

Charles Eckles, Eastman, Georgia—September 10, 1991

Fred Miller, Jr., Eastman, Georgia—September 10, 1991

Senator Hugh Gillis, Soperton, Georgia—September 17, 1991

Emmett Barnes, Macon, Georgia—October 3, 1991

W. S. (Bill) Stuckey, Jr., Eastman, Georgia—November 3, 1991

Lynda Stuckey Franklin, Eastman, Georgia—April 15, 1992 and May 11, 1993

Beverly Stuckey Franklin, Mercer University's Walter F. George School of Law, Macon, Georgia—October 8, 1992

Rev. J. B. (Jake) Hutchinson, Richmond Hill, Georgia—August 20, 1993

Telephone interviews:

Billy Stuckey, III, Augusta, Georgia—July 8, 1992

Stephanie Stuckey, Atlanta, Georgia—May, 1992

Stuart Stuckey, St. Simons Island, Georgia—May, 1992

Russell Dean Franklin, III, Monroe, Georgia—November 12, 1992

Information obtained by Lynda Stuckey Franklin by telephone May 11, 1993 from Mrs. Sylvia Rubin and Mrs. Elizabeth Harrell, Eastman, Georgia

Research, Sources:

Genealogical information, Anne Stuckey Clarke, Atlanta, who shared materials gleaned from a number of sources.

Washington Memorial Library Archives.

World Book Encyclopedia

The Timetables of History, Simon & Schuster

War, Economy and Society—1933—1945—Alan S. Milward

The People's Chronology, Holt, Rinehart & Winston

Chronicle of the 20th Century, Chronicle Publications

The Macon Telegraph, May 5, 1992—"50 Years Ago"

Georgia Official & Statistical Register 1931 – 1975

Georgia Population of Counties from Earliest Census to 1970

Georgia—Historical and Industrial by the Department of Agriculture

History of Dodge County by Mrs. Wilton Philip Cobb, The Reprint Company, Spartanburg, S. C.

Dodge County Newspaper Clippings by Ted Evans, Vols, IV, V, VI, VII, VIII, IX and X

Who's Who in the South and Southwest—Eleventh Edition

Memoirs of Georgia—published by the Atlanta Historical Society, 1895

Stuckey Scrapbook, Eastman, Georgia

The Atlanta Journal-Constitution Magazine—Article by Ellen Fort Grissett, date omitted—1977

The Atlanta Journal – Constitution—December 17, 1958

The Times Journal, Eastman, Georgia, Special Stuckey edition, March 4, 1953

Times Journal Spotlight, Eastman, Georgia. January 13, 1977

The Macon Telegraph and News—September 22, 1957 and October 19, 1949

Candy Industry and Confectioner's Journal, December 6, 1960

Sweetalk—Stuckey Newsletter

Newsweek, July 6, 1953

Investors' Reader—December 18, 1963

The Courier Herald, Dublin, Georgia—November 15, 1983

The Houston Chronicle, Perry, Georgia—December 2, 1984

Goodyear Triangle—September 18, 1962

The New Yorker—March 9, 1963

Sunset Magazine—April 1963

Southern Post—April 21, 1960

The Peanut Journal and *Nut World*—undated

Georgia Department of Commerce Newsletter—October 25, 1950

Cross and Crescent—June 1975

Trux—December 1962

Business Week—June 30, Year Unknown—1960s

Hospitality—March 1964

Middle Georgia Magazine, article by William J. Steele

Advertisements for Stuckey's: *Reader's Digest, Holiday, Look, Saturday Evening Post, Better Homes and Gardens, Newsweek*

Stuckey: The Biography of Williamson Sylvester Stuckey
by Elizabeth McCants Drinnon

Published by Mercer University Press
October 1997

Book design by Marc A. Jolley.

Camera-ready pages composed on a Macintosh
Performa 6300CD, via Microsoft Word 6.0.1.
Text font: Book Antiqua 11/12.
Printed and bound in the United States.
Cased and covered with cloth, smyth-sewn, and
printed on acid-free paper.